Kindergarten

MIND BUILDING MATH

Developing Skills Using Critical Thinking

Written by Christine Broz
Illustrated by Eric Cardinale

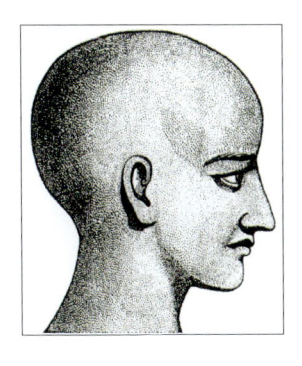

© 2004
THE CRITICAL THINKING COMPANY
(BRIGHT MINDS™)
www.CriticalThinking.com
P.O. Box 1610 • Seaside • CA 93955-1610
Phone 800-458-4849 • FAX 831-393-3277
ISBN 0-89455-844-7
This book is non-reproducible.

TABLE OF CONTENTS

Introduction 3

Numbers & Operations
Counting 1
Ordering Numbers 14
Ordinal Numbers 18
Comparing Numbers 22
Number Words 23
Comparing Sets 24
Estimating 36
Grouping Objects 39
Adding/Subtracting 46
Fractions Whole/Half 70
Counting by 5s and 10s 75
Coin Value 80

Algebra
Extending Patterns 87
Ordering Objects by Size 96

Geometry
Comparing 2D & 3D Shapes 98
Shape Attributes 105
Combining and Sorting Shapes 109
Spatial Position 112
Directions 115

Measurement
Comparing Length, Weight, Volume 120
Measuring 126
Telling Time 129
Days of Week 132

Data Analysis
Using Data & Graphing 135
Using Venn Diagram 143

Answers 146

Skills Matrices 154

Introduction

Mind Building Math is a supplement designed to develop a student's critical thinking skills in mathematics. It is based on the current math standards developed by the National Council of Teachers of Mathematics and aligns with state math standards. These fun, thought-provoking activities promote problem solving, logic, and observation, skills that prepare students for higher-level math and early assessment tests.

Mind Building Math contains the following sections: Numbers and Operations, Algebra, Geometry, Measurement, and Data Analysis. Each activity focuses on a particular skill listed at the top of the page. Within each unit, the activities progress in difficulty. These engaging story problems and puzzles require students to count with understanding, compare, classify, match, draw, sort, look for patterns, interpret, and analyze using visual clues.

How to Use this Book

The directions for each activity in *Mind Building Math* should be read to students individually or in small groups. These activities should not be attempted by a student as independent work. What is most important is the quality of interaction between you and the child. After completing an activity, ask your students how they solved the problem and see if they can identify other strategies for solving the problem. The skills matrices at the back of the book identify the mathematical standards and thinking skills used in each activity.

Some images used herein were obtained from © 2003–2004 www.clipart.com and from IMSI's Master Clips® Premium Image Collection, 1895 Francisco Blvd. East, San Rafael, CA 94901-5506, USA.

Mind Building Math — Counting

Help the kitten find its way to the yarn. Circle the numbers in order from 1 to 15, then draw a line to connect the numbers.

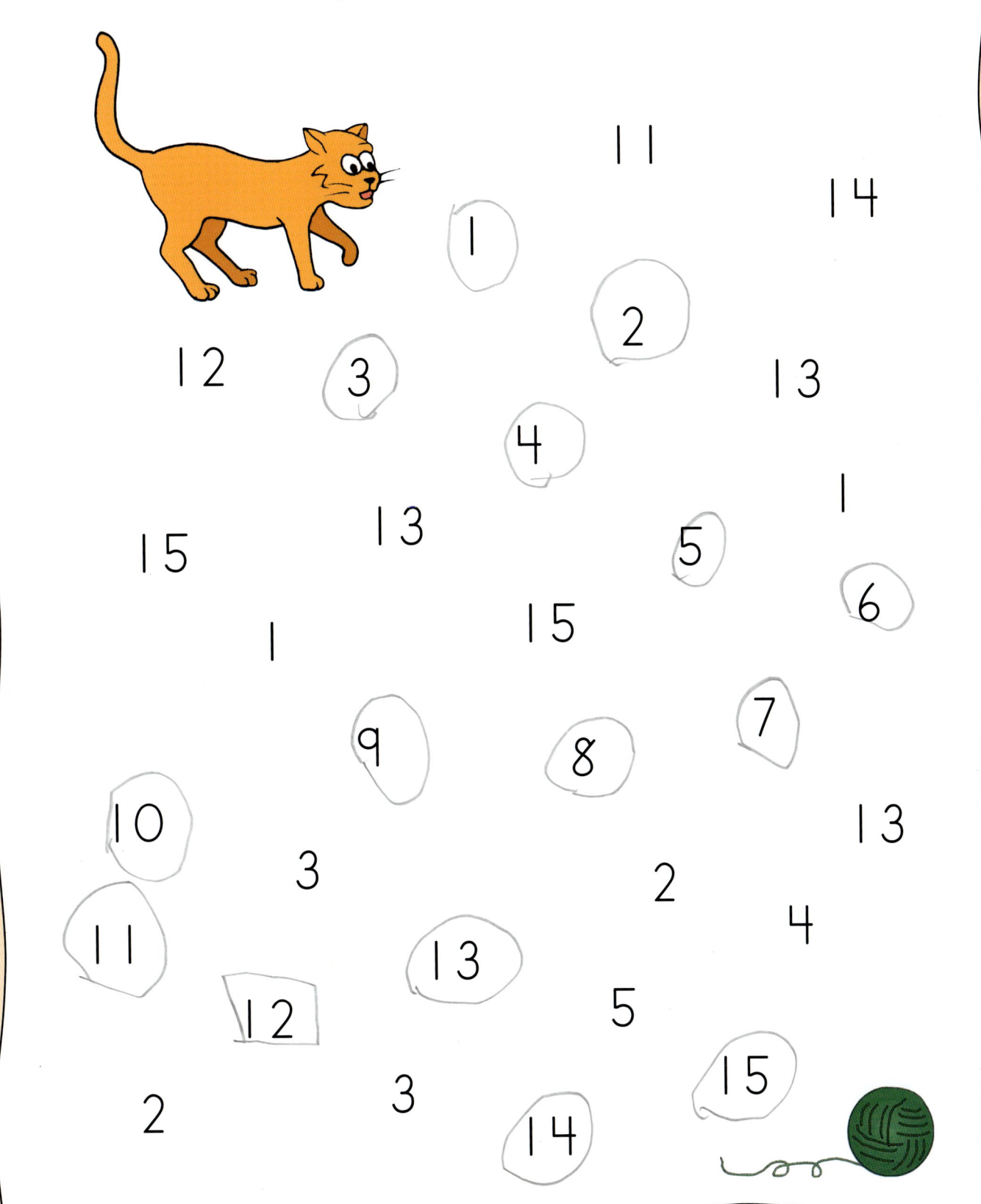

Counting   Mind Building Math

1. Circle what Rabbit will find if she jumps on 5 spaces.

   🥕   🥬   🍅   🫛

2. Circle what Rabbit will find if she jumps on 7 spaces.

   🥕   🥬   🍅   🫛

3. On how many spaces does Rabbit
   need to jump to find 2 tomatoes? _____

4. On how many spaces does Rabbit
   need to jump to find 3 carrots? _____

Count the total number of dots on each domino and draw a line to connect the dominoes in order from 1 to 10.

Counting   Mind Building Math

1. Circle what Frog will catch if he lands on space 8.

2. Circle what Frog will catch if he lands on space 16.

3. On how many spaces does Frog need to jump to catch the second fly? ____

4. On how many spaces does Frog need to jump to catch 2 ants and 1 spider? ____

Mind Building Math

Counting

Help the fish find its way to the fish bowl. Circle the numbers in order from 15 to 30, then draw a line to connect the numbers.

15   11   16
     28
12   3   17
     18
     14   6   12
19
          21
     20   22
25   23
          24
  9   13
26   27   2
     17   28
           16
        29
           20   30
     18
        11

© 2004 The Critical Thinking Company • www.CriticalThinking.com • 800-458-4849

5

Counting   Mind Building Math

Eric likes to jump in puddles and make big splashes.

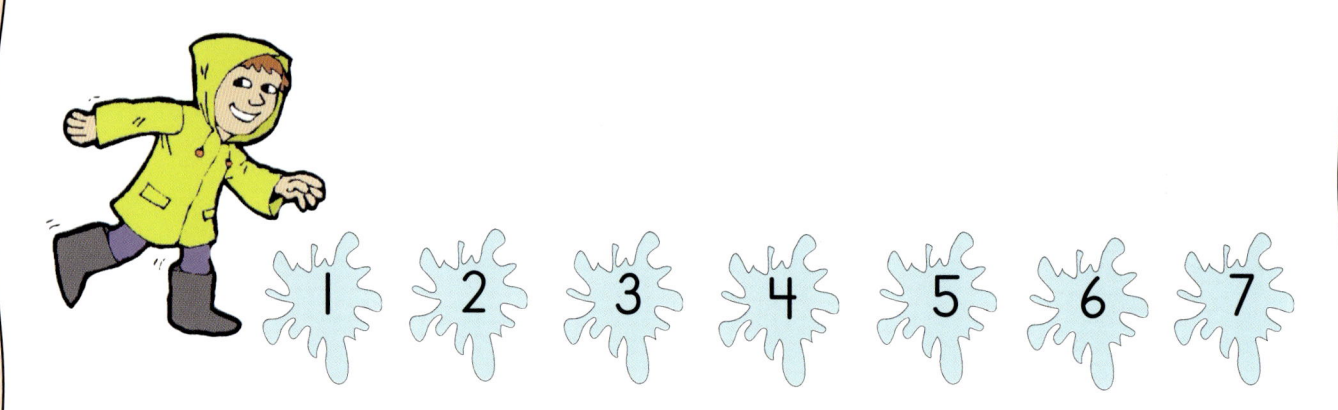

1 2 3 4 5 6 7

1. If Eric is in puddle 1 and jumps forward
   3 puddles, which puddle will he land in? 4

2. If Eric is in puddle 2 and jumps forward
   2 puddles, which puddle will he land in? 4

3. If Eric is in puddle 3 and jumps forward
   4 puddles, which puddle will he land in? ___

4. If Eric is in puddle 4 and jumps forward
   1 puddle, which puddle will he land in? 5

5. Eric skips every other puddle. If he starts
   in puddle 1, which puddle will he end in? 7

Mind Building Math Counting

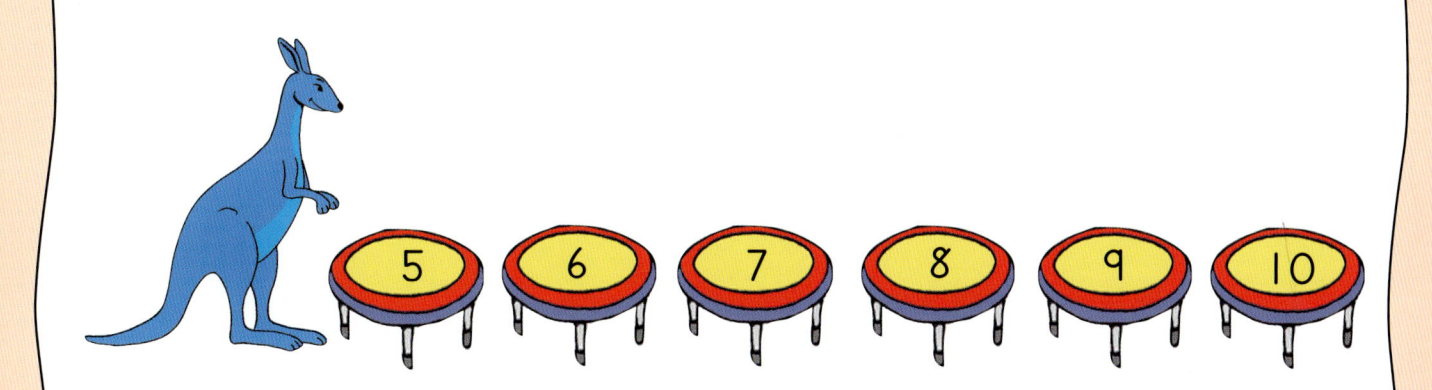

1. If Blue Kangaroo hops to 7 and then hops back 1 space, which number will he land on? ____

2. If Blue Kangaroo hops to 9 and then hops back 3 spaces, which number will he land on? ____

3. If Blue Kangaroo hops to 10, and then hops back 2 spaces, which number will he land on? ____

4. If Blue Kangaroo hops to 8 and then hops back 3 spaces, which number will he land on? ____

5. If Blue Kangaroo hops to 10 and then hops back 4 spaces, which number will he land on? ____

Counting   Mind Building Math

Little Dragon loved to swim in the lake on lazy afternoons. He was often lonely and thought it would be fun to swim with friends. He sent out a message to all the dragons in the nearby land to come for a swimming party. When the guests arrived, Little Dragon was surprised! Some of the dragons had three heads, some of them had two heads, and some of them had one head. However, each dragon had only one body and one tail.

1. Look at the picture on the next page. How many dragons come to the swimming party, not including the little dragon? _____

2. Circle the number of party hats Little Dragon needs for the party guests in the lake.

3. How many tail floats does Little Dragon need for the party guests? _____

4. How many cookies does Little Dragon need so that all his guests have at least one? _____ Explain your thinking.

Mind Building Math   Counting

Little Dragon

Counting   Mind Building Math

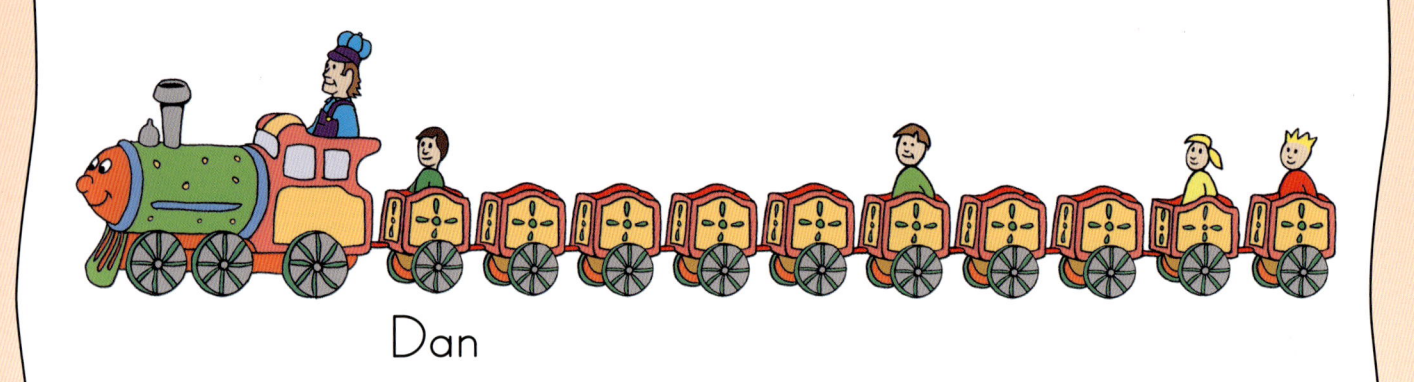

Dan

Dan is sitting in seat one, the first seat behind the train engineer. The train engineer asks him to move to the first empty seat after seat five.

1. Write 5 below seat number five.

2. Circle the seat Dan will move to.

3. How many children are on the train? _____

4. If five more children get on the train, how many children will then be on the train? _____
   Draw the children on the train to help find the answer.

5. Now, how many empty seats are left on the train? _____

Mind Building Math

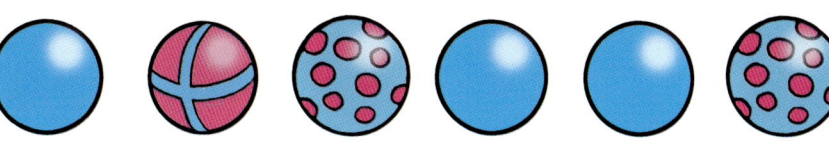

Counting

The beads above fell off the necklaces below. Draw each bead on the necklace it came from. Then write how many beads are on each necklace you fixed.

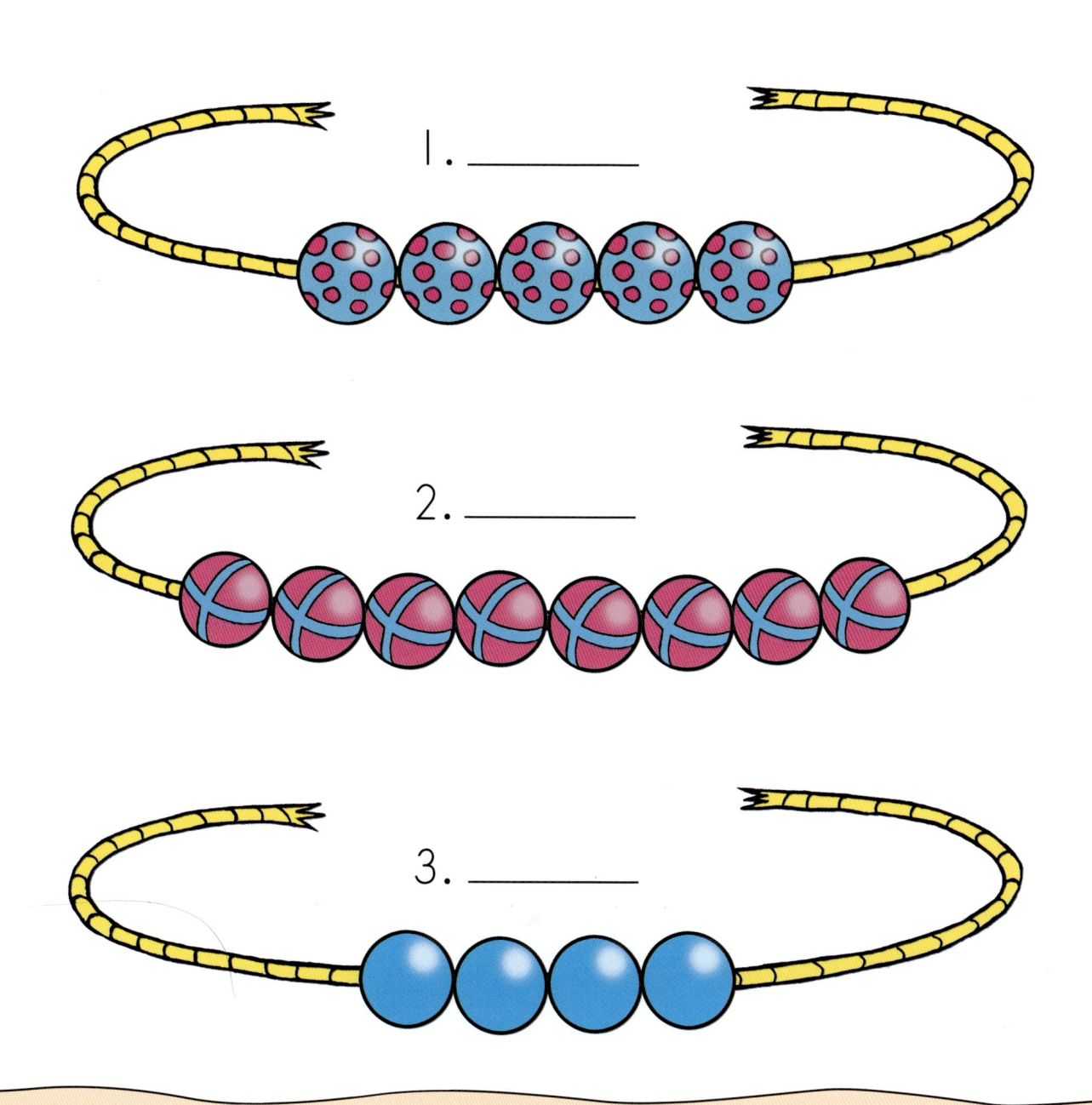

1. _____

2. _____

3. _____

© 2004 The Critical Thinking Company • www.CriticalThinking.com • 800-458-4849

Counting   Mind Building Math

David and Jen are building a big sand castle at the beach.
David wants to put a flag on the top of every tall building.

1. Draw the flags on the castle.
   How many flags does he need? _____

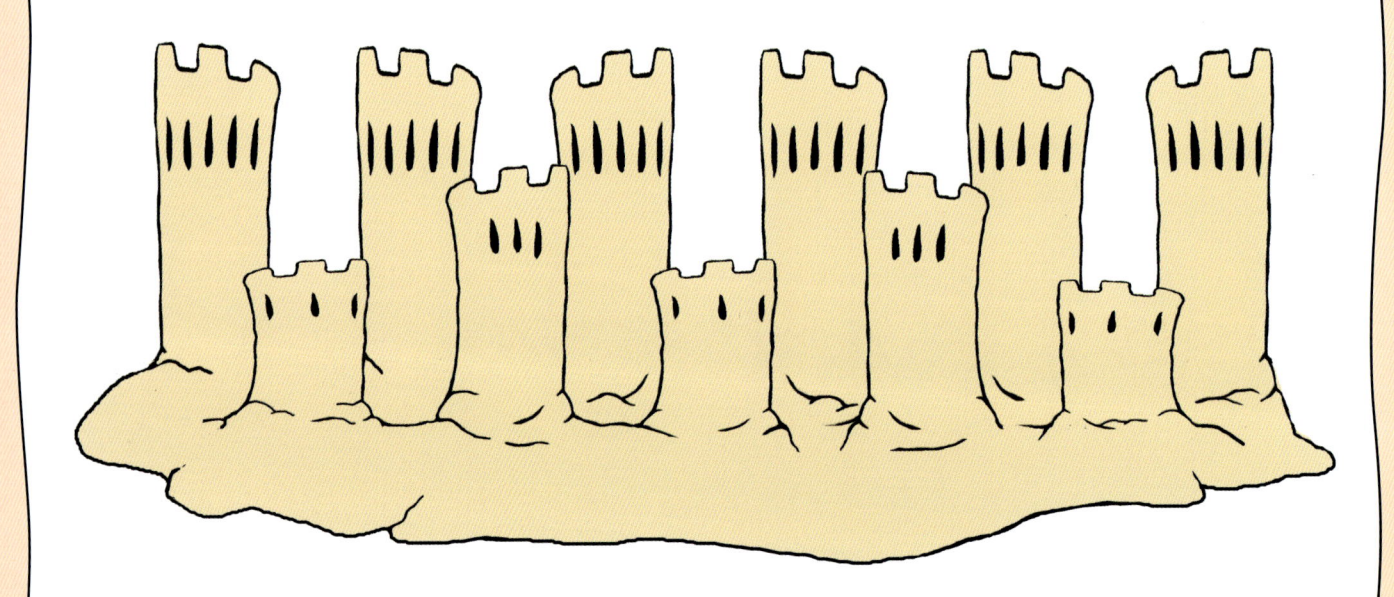

Jen wants to decorate the shortest
buildings with 2 shells each.

2. Draw the shells on the castle.
   How many shells does she need to collect? _____

3. How many buildings are there in all? _____

4. If the water comes in and knocks
   down 5 buildings, how many will be left? _____

Mind Building Math

Counting

Pat wanted to get some gumballs for her friends. Two gumballs cost 1¢.

Draw the gumballs beside each coin, then number them. How many gumballs can she buy with the coins below? 10

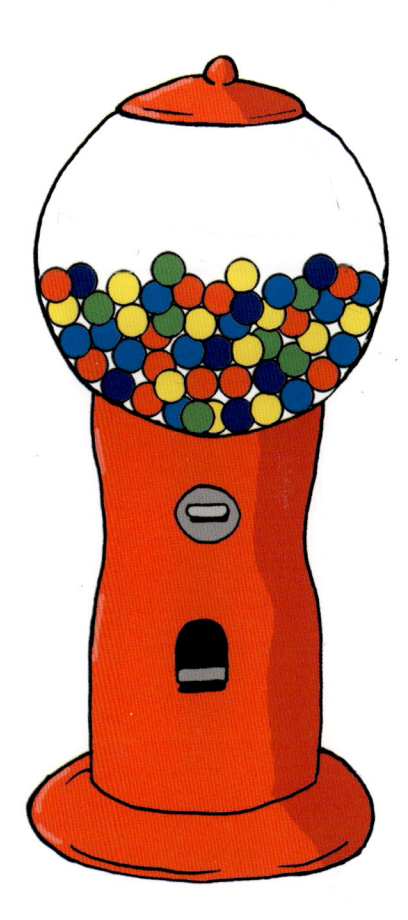

Ordering Numbers

Mind Building Math

Write each group of numbers on the lines in order from smallest to largest.

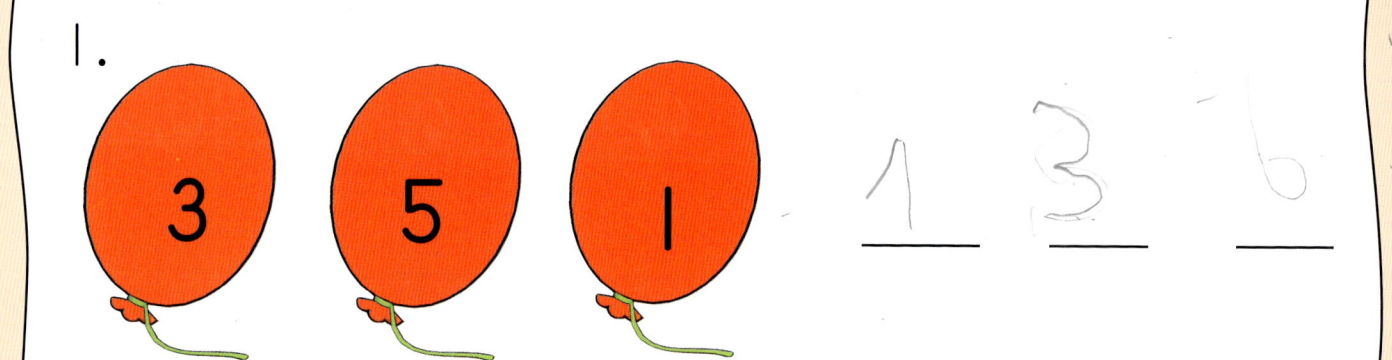

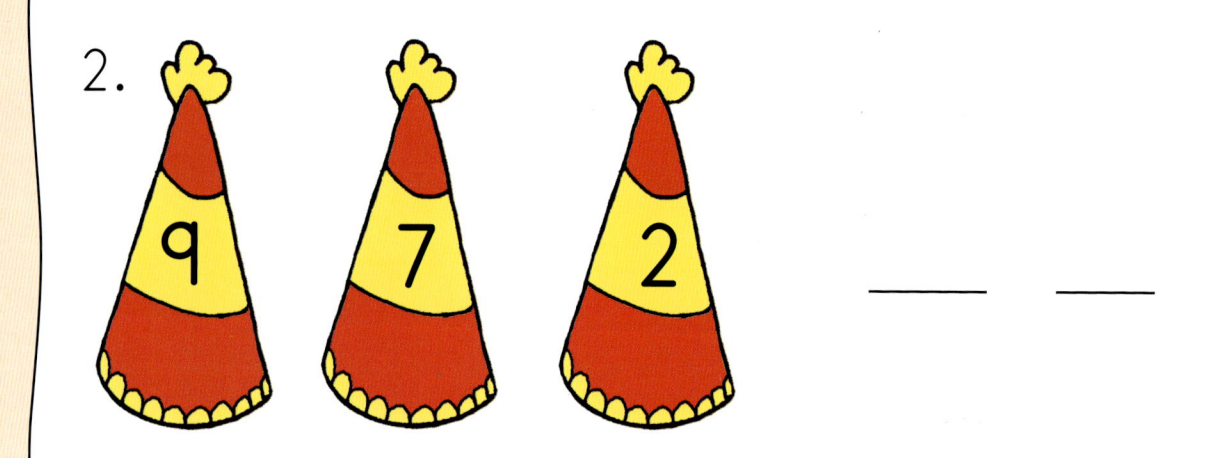

1. 3 5 1   1 3 6

2. 9 7 2   ___ ___ ___

3. 8 5 10   ___ ___ ___

Mind Building Math

Ordering Numbers

1. I'm thinking of a number that is after 1 and before 3. What's my number? _____

2. I'm thinking of a number that is after 4 and before 6. What's my number? _____

3. I'm thinking of a number that is before 9 and after 7. What's my number? _____

4. How many elephants have a number that is before 7? _____

© 2004 The Critical Thinking Company • www.CriticalThinking.com • 800-458-4849

Ordering Numbers

Mind Building Math

Write each group of numbers on the lines in order from smallest to largest.

1. 12 17 15   ___ ___ ___

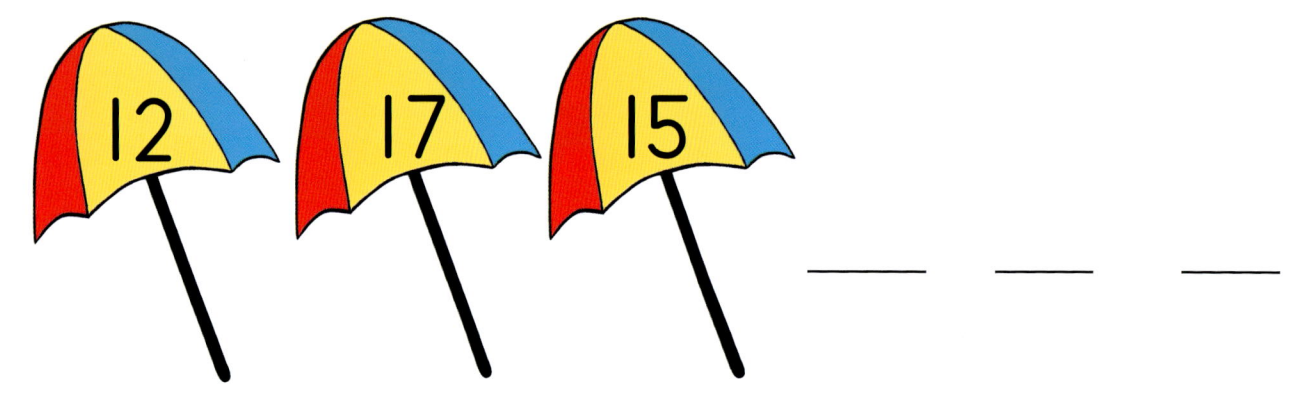

2. 26 22 20   ___ ___ ___

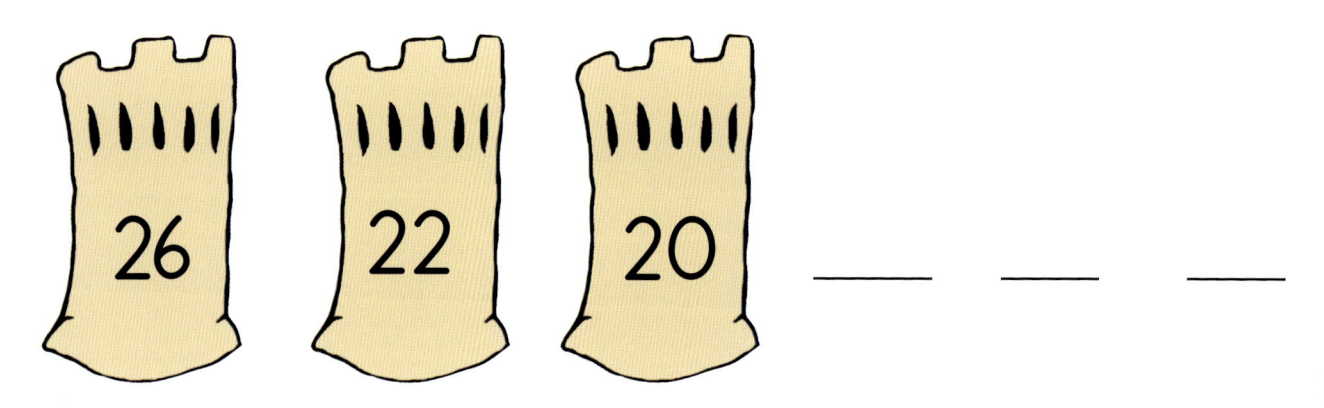

3. 28 29 23   ___ ___ ___

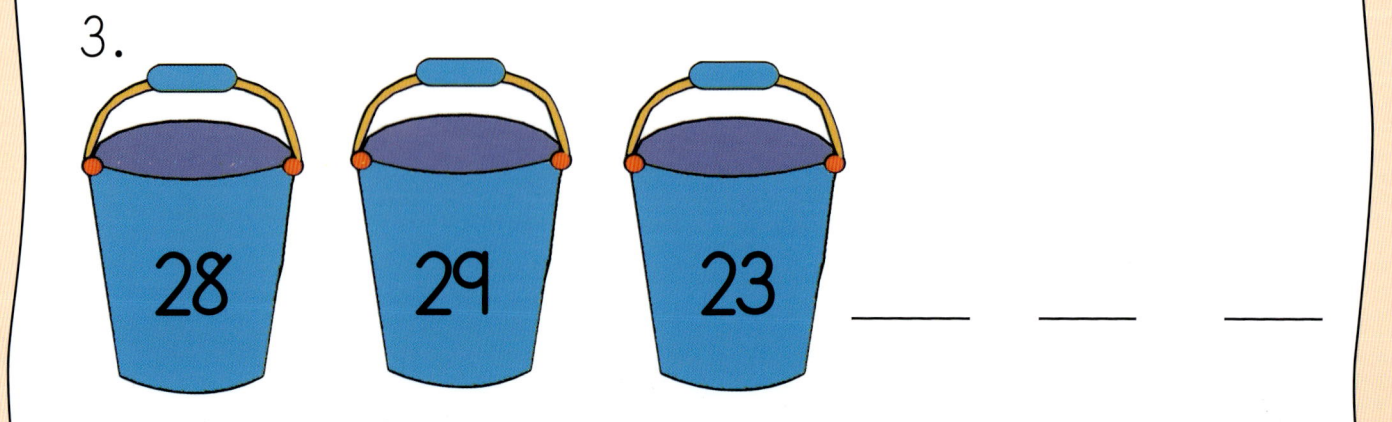

Mind Building Math

Ordering Numbers

1. The racing rabbits are lined up in order from the smallest number to the largest number. Write the correct number from the box on each rabbit.

| 3 7 5 9 |

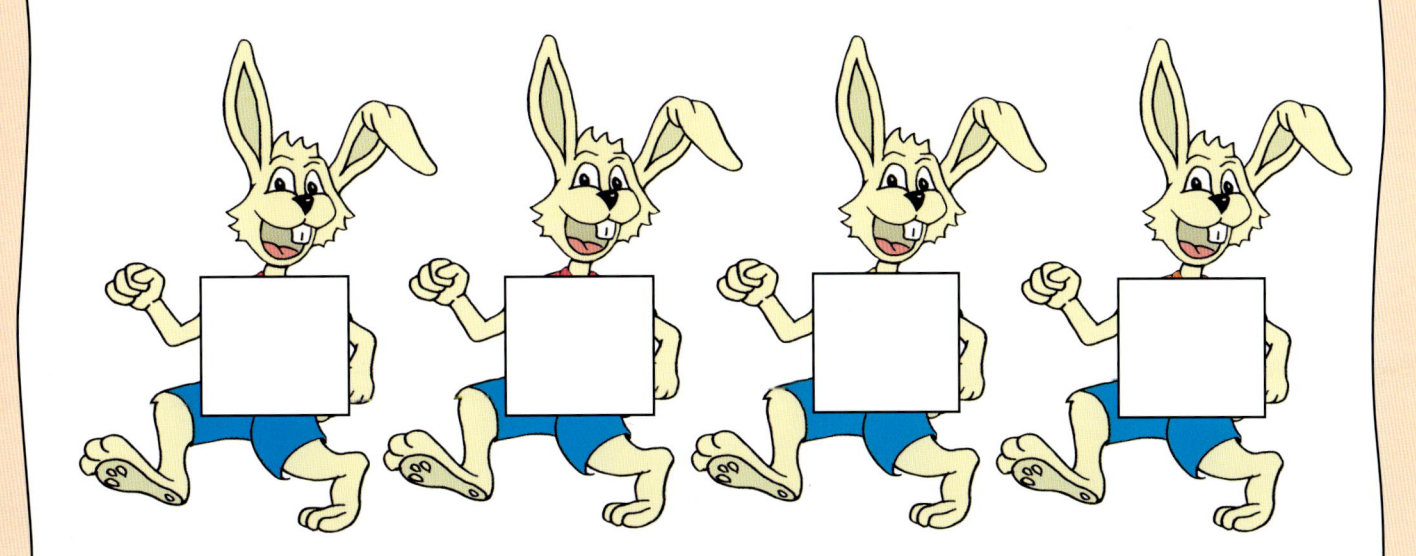

2. The race cars are lined up in order from the largest number to the smallest number. Write the correct number from the box on each car.

| 14 19 12 16 |

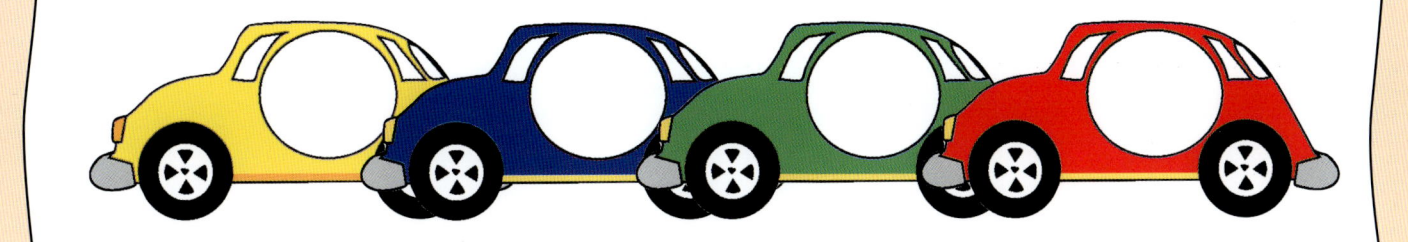

© 2004 The Critical Thinking Company • www.CriticalThinking.com • 800-458-4849

Ordinal Numbers

Mind Building Math

1 2 3 4 5 6 7 8 9 10

1. I'm thinking of a number that comes after the third number but before the fifth number. What's my number? _____

2. I'm thinking of a number that comes after the fourth number but before the sixth number. What's my number? _____

3. I am thinking of a number that comes before the third number but after the first number. What's my number? _____

4. I am thinking of a number that comes after the seventh number but before the ninth number. What's my number? _____

Mind Building Math

Ordinal Numbers

Yuki put the shapes in a row. She asked Saul to point to the third shape in the row. Saul wasn't sure at which end he should start counting.

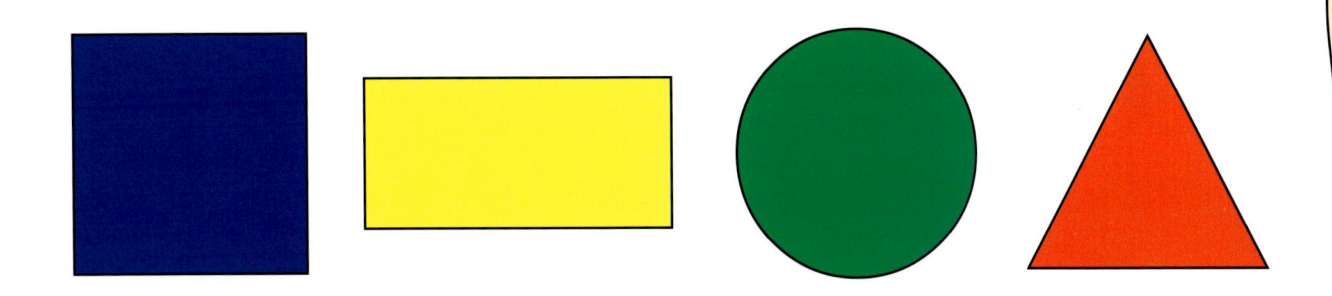

1. If the square is first, which shape is third?

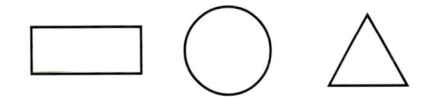

2. If the rectangle is second, which shape is fourth?

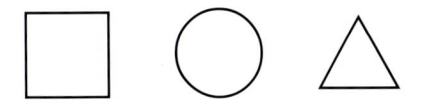

3. If the square is the last shape, which is the first shape?

4. If the second shape is the circle, which shape is third?

Ordinal Numbers																																		Mind Building Math

The teacher asked the kids to line up to go to lunch. They weren't sure which door they would go out.

Reese   Lucy   Ned   Lee   Wendy

1. If they go out the black door, who will be first?
   Reese   Wendy

2. If Lucy is second in line, who is fourth?
   Lee   Wendy

3. If Reese is last in line, which door will they go out?
   black   white

4. If they go out the black door, which will Lucy be?
   2nd   3rd   4th

Mind Building Math • Ordinal Numbers

1. I am thinking of a number that comes after the second monkey but before the third monkey. What's my number? _____

2. I'm thinking of a number that comes after the second snake but before the third snake. What's my number? _____

3. I'm thinking of a number that comes after the fourth monkey but before the fifth monkey. What's my number? _____

4. I am thinking of a number that comes before the fourth snake but after the third snake. What's my number? _____

Comparing Numbers — Mind Building Math

A magician had three hats. He pulled some bunnies out of each hat. In each group, put an X on the bunny with the largest number and circle the bunny with the smallest number.

Group 1: 13, 45, 6, 8, 34

Group 2: 29, 34, 17, 12, 35

Group 3: 40, 82, 73, 65, 51

Mind Building Math Number Words

1 one	2 two	3 three	4 four	5 five
6 six	7 seven	8 eight	9 nine	10 ten

Below, draw a line from each number word to the box with the same number of dots. Use the chart above for clues.

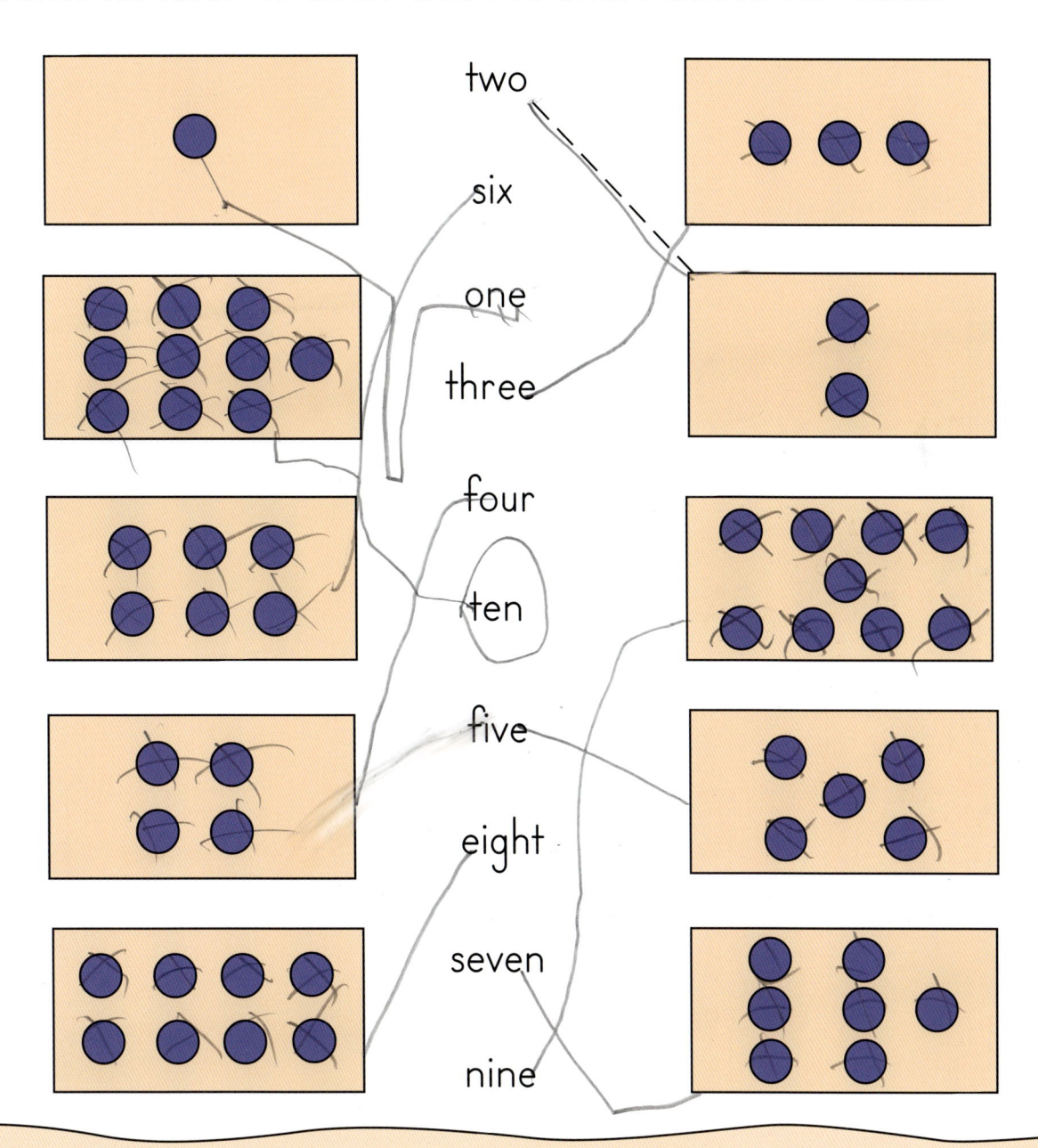

two
six
one
three
four
ten
five
eight
seven
nine

Comparing Sets   Mind Building Math

Draw lines to match up the objects in each group.
Then tell how many more the larger set has.

1. How many more? 2

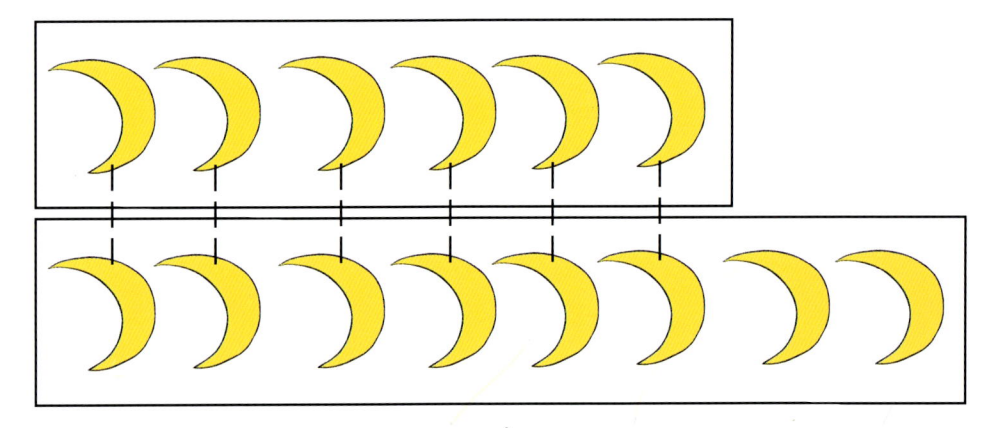

2. How many more? 4

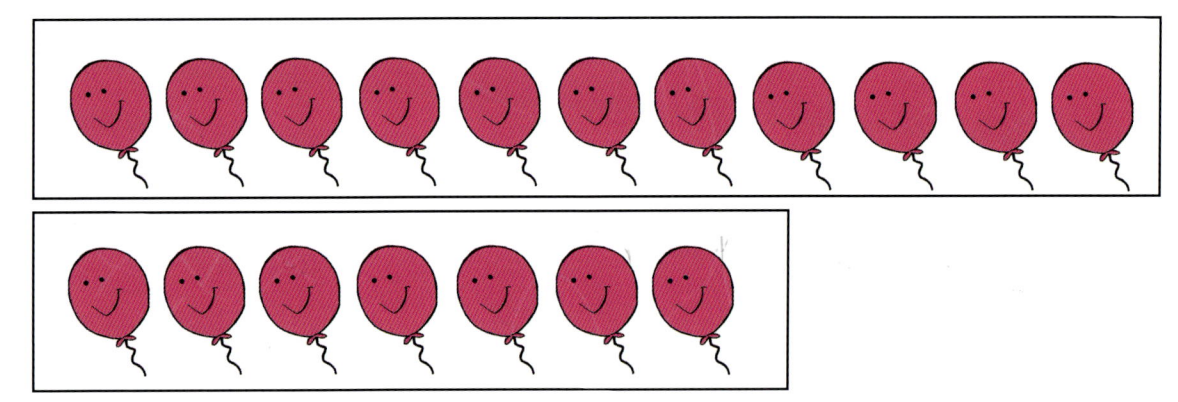

3. How many more? 5

Mind Building Math

Comparing Sets

Draw the eggs that belong to each chicken.
   The yellow chicken has 5 eggs.
   The spotted chicken has 8 eggs.
   The black chicken has 6 eggs.

1. Circle the chicken that has the most eggs.

2. How many more eggs does the black chicken have than the yellow chicken? __1__

3. Count how many eggs there are altogether. __19__

Comparing Sets

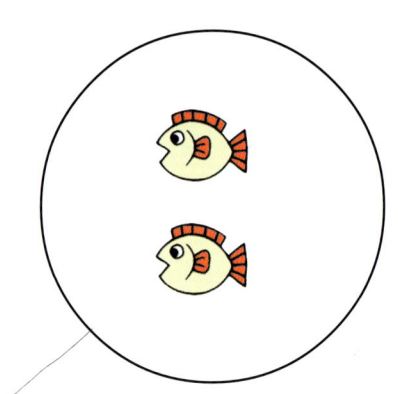

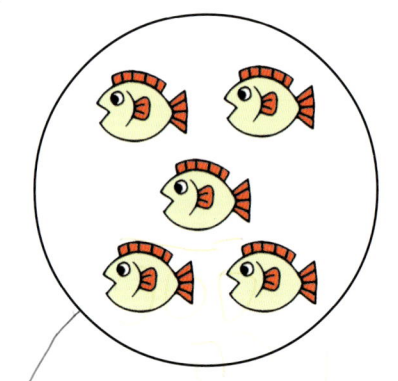

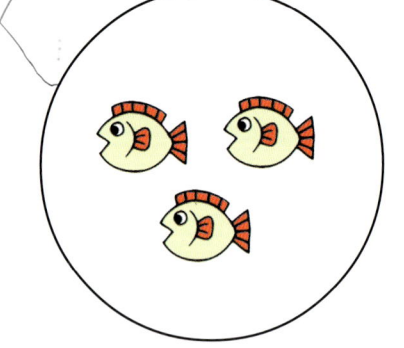

Mind Building Math

Draw a line from each penguin to its lunch.

This penguin ate 3 fish.

This penguin ate 1 fish less than the penguin above.

This penguin ate 2 fish more than the penguin at the top.

Mind Building Math

Comparing Sets

Draw a line from each dog to its bones.

Spot has 9 bones.

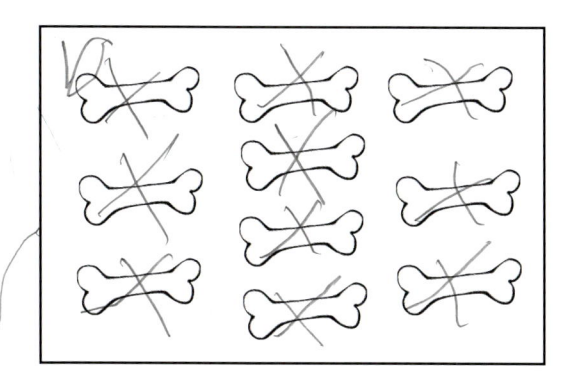

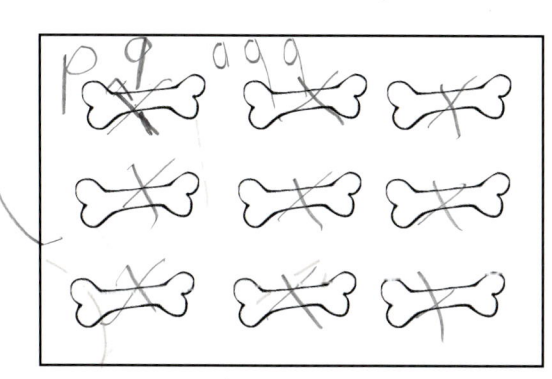

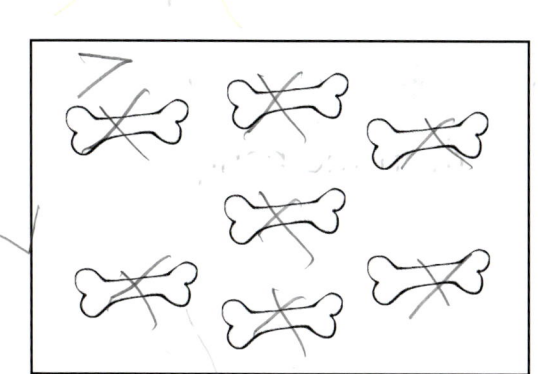

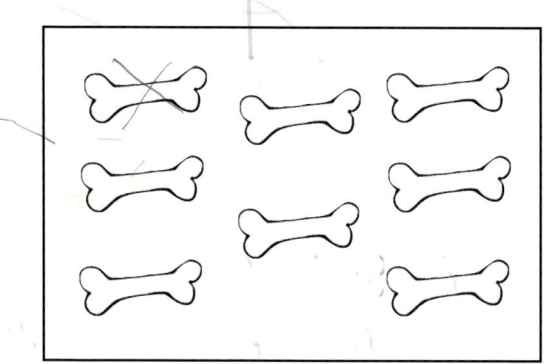

Mocha has 2 bones less than Spot.

Boots has 3 more bones than Mocha.

© 2004 The Critical Thinking Company • www.CriticalThinking.com • 800-458-4849

27

Comparing Sets   Mind Building Math

1. Count the objects in the group below and in the groups on the next page. Write how many are in each group.

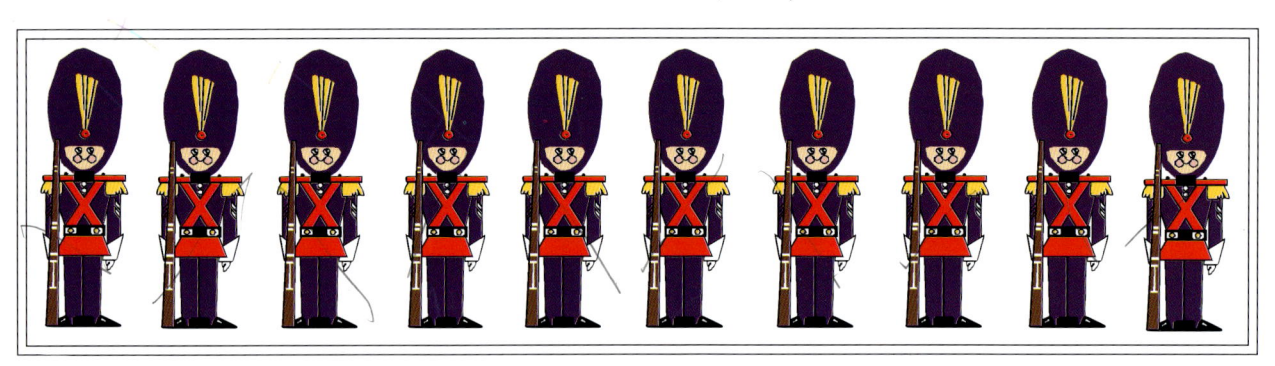

How many? __10__

2. Which group has the same number of objects as the toy soldier group?

3. Which group has one more than the toy soldier group?

4. Which group has one less than the toy soldier group?

28   © 2004 The Critical Thinking Company • www.CriticalThinking.com • 800-458-4849

Mind Building Math

Comparing Sets

How many? 11

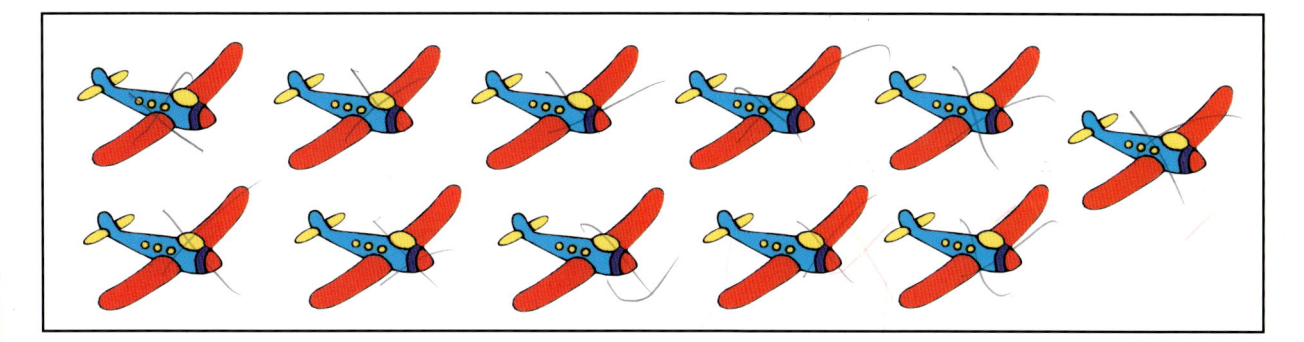

How many? 9

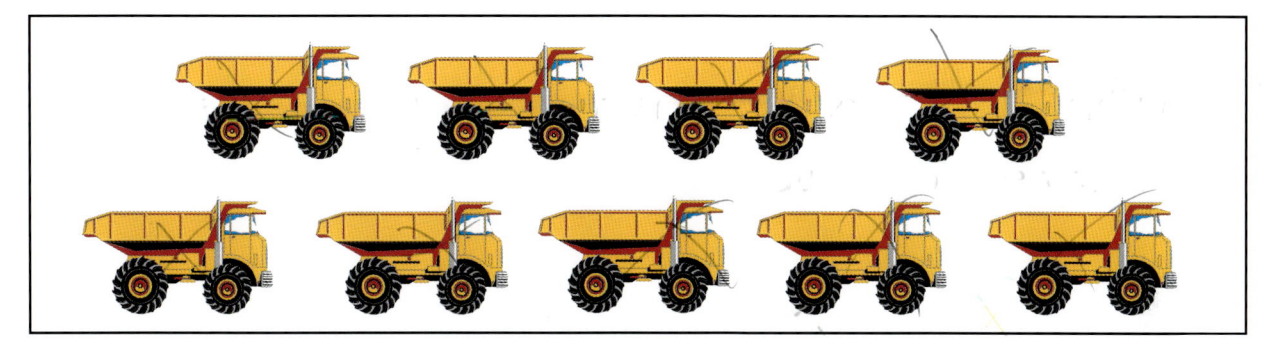

How many? 10

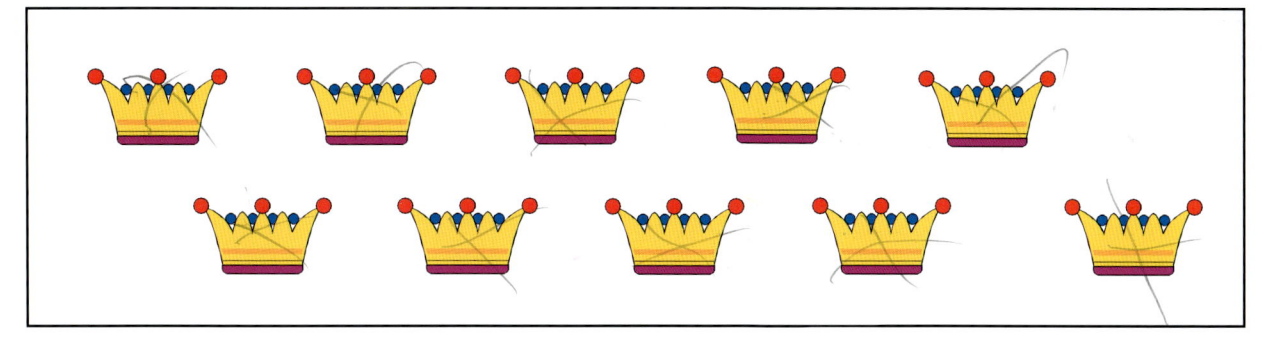

29

Comparing Sets

Mind Building Math

1. Count the objects in the group below and in the groups on the next page. Write how many are in each group.

How many? _____

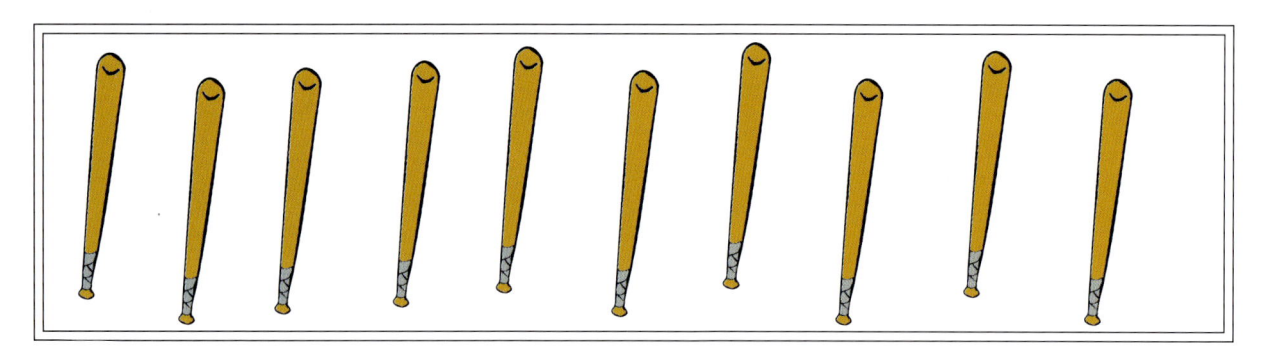

2. Which group has the same number of objects as the group of bats?

3. Which group has one more than the group of bats?

4. Which group has one less than the group of bats?

30 © 2004 The Critical Thinking Company • www.CriticalThinking.com • 800-458-4849

Mind Building Math

Comparing Sets

How many? _____

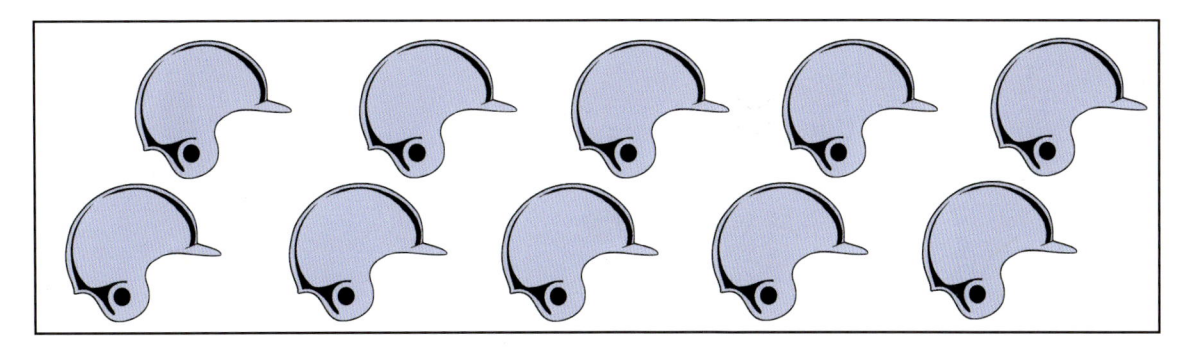

How many? _____

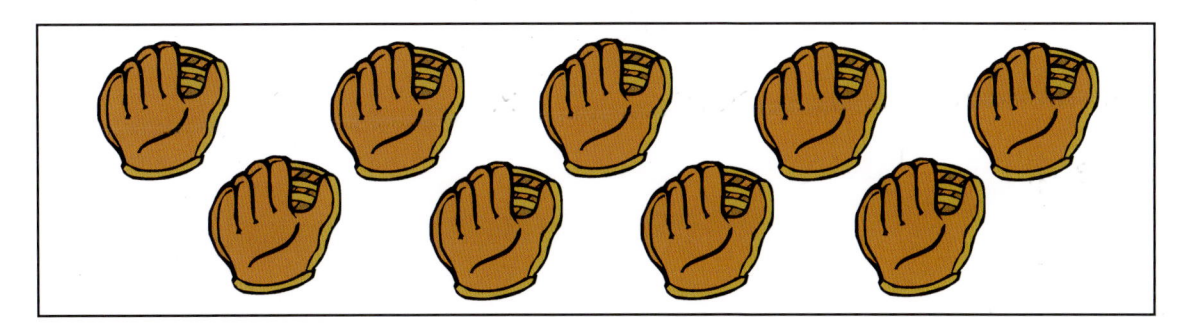

How many? _____

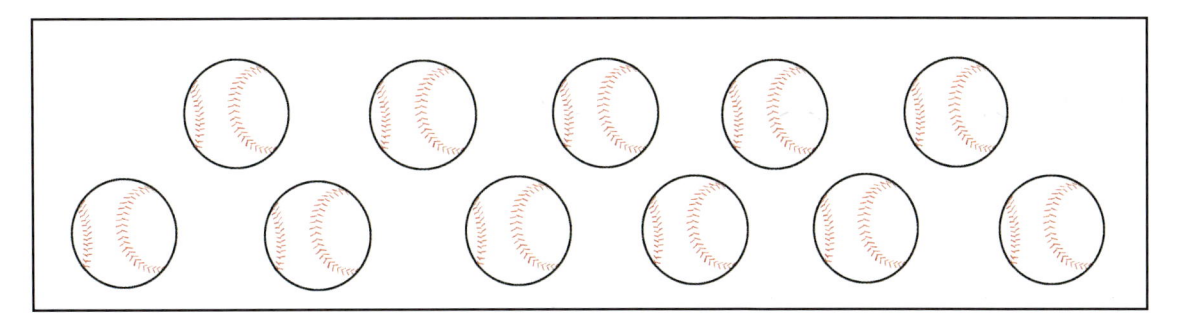

Comparing Sets   Mind Building Math

_____   _____
 Bobo   Jojo

        _____
         Coco

1. Count the boxes each clown is holding.
   Under each clown, write the number of boxes.

2. Which clown is holding the most boxes? _____

3. How many fewer boxes
   does Bobo have than Coco? _____

4. How many more boxes
   does Jojo have than Bobo? _____

Mind Building Math

Comparing Sets

Use the clues to find which row of candy belongs to each child. Draw a line to match each child with his or her candy.

Deb has 2 green and 3 red.

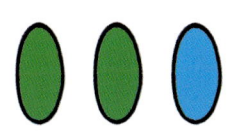

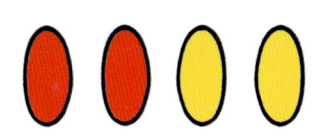

Megan has one more than Deb.

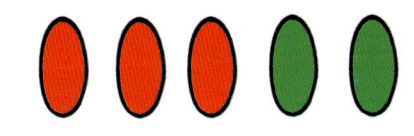

Tim has 3 less than Megan.

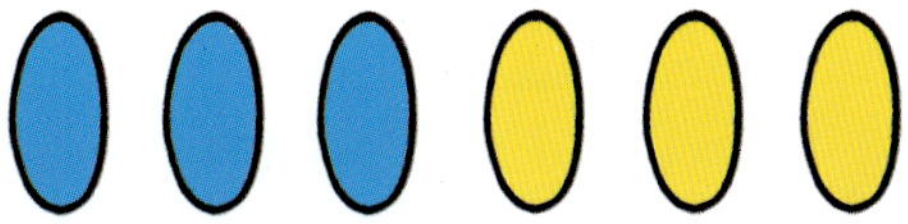

© 2004 The Critical Thinking Company • www.CriticalThinking.com • 800-458-4849

Comparing Sets

Mind Building Math

Use the clues below to find out which row of candy belongs to each child. Draw a line to match each child with his or her candy.

Pat has 3 of each color.

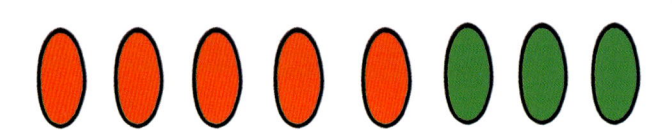

Sue has 1 less than Pat.

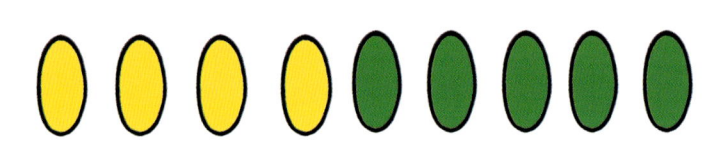

Mike has 2 more than Sue.

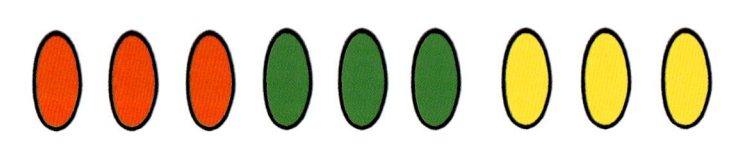

Jen has 1 less than Mike.

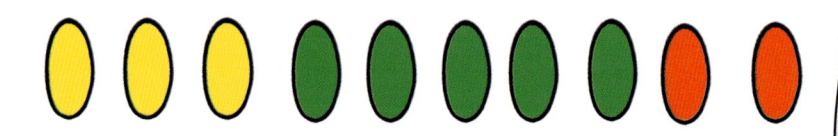

Mind Building Math

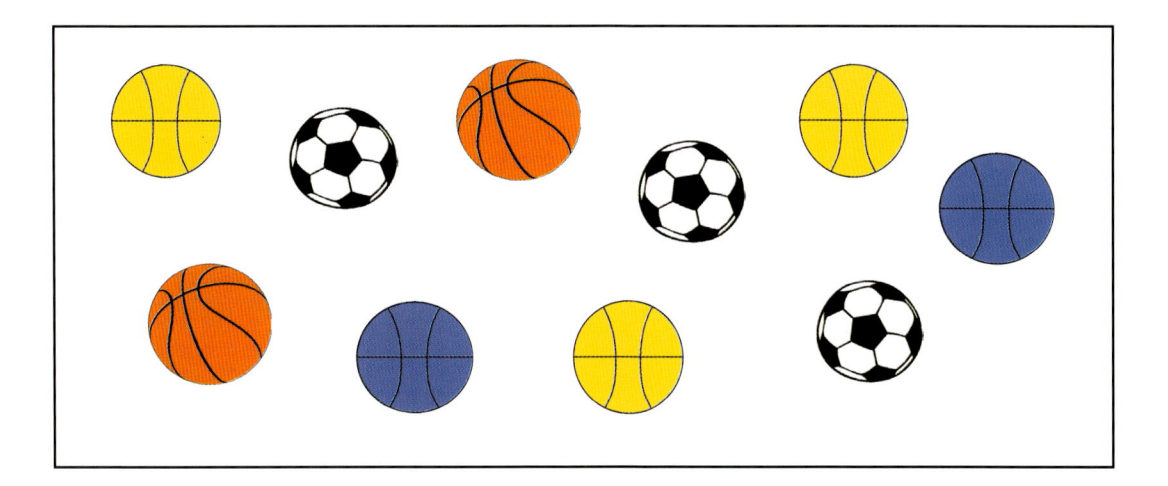

Comparing Sets

A kindergarten and a first grade class must share the balls in the box. The kindergarten class takes these balls out.

1. In the box, cross off the balls the kindergarten class took. How many balls are left in the box for the first grade class? _____

2. Which classroom has more?   kindergarten   first

3. How many of each ball are left in the box?

___ ___ ___ ___

© 2004 The Critical Thinking Company • www.CriticalThinking.com • 800-458-4849

Estimating   Mind Building Math

1. If this jar has 15 beads, estimate how many beads are in the full jar.

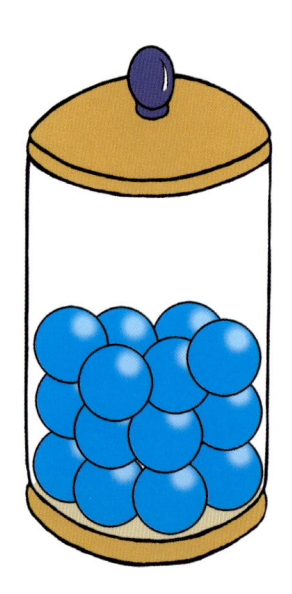

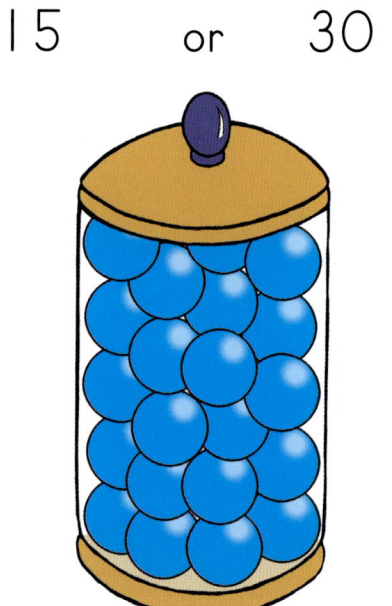

   15   or   30

2. If this jar has 40 candies, estimate how many candies are in the full jar.

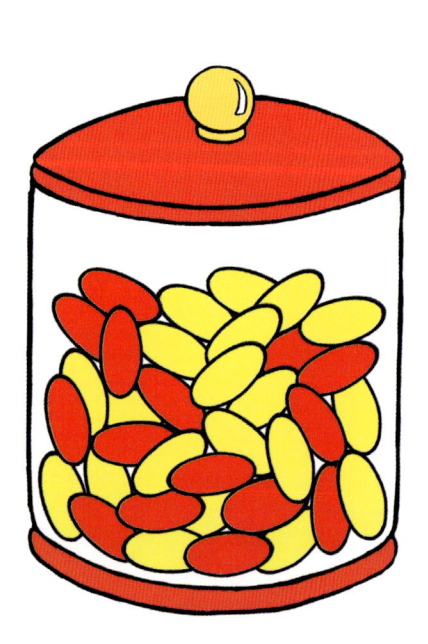

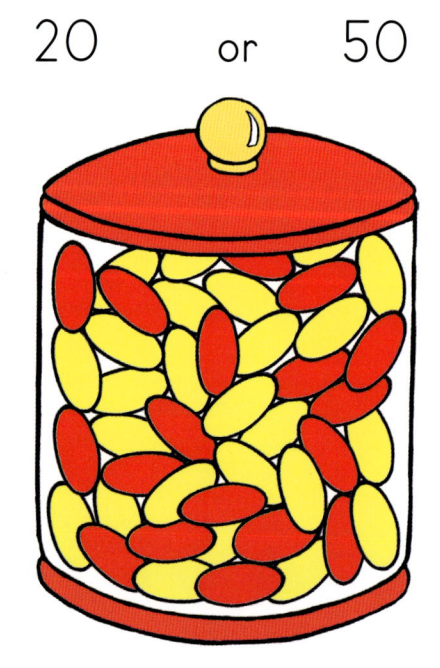

   20   or   50

Mind Building Math

Estimating

Some fish in the tank are red, some are yellow, and some are both colors.

1. Without counting, circle the kind below you think there are the most of.

2. Now, count how many of each kind of fish are in the tank. Write the number of each kind on the line.

Estimating

Mind Building Math

This is a group of 5 ladybugs.

1. Without counting, estimate about how many ladybugs are in each group below. Circle the number that is closest to your guess.

20   50   10   30

_____   _____

2. Now, count how many ladybugs are in each group and write the number on the line.

Mind Building Math

Grouping Objects

The picture above shows how many clowns can fit in one car.

1. Draw a circle around each group of clowns that will fit in one car.

2. How many of the cars below will the clowns fill? _____

Grouping Objects　　　　　　　　　　　　　　　　　　　　　　Mind Building Math

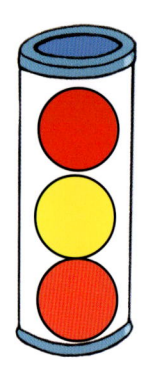

1. How many yellow balls are in the can? _____

2. How many red balls are in the can? _____

3. Circle each set of balls that would fill a can like the one above. How many cans would they fill? _____

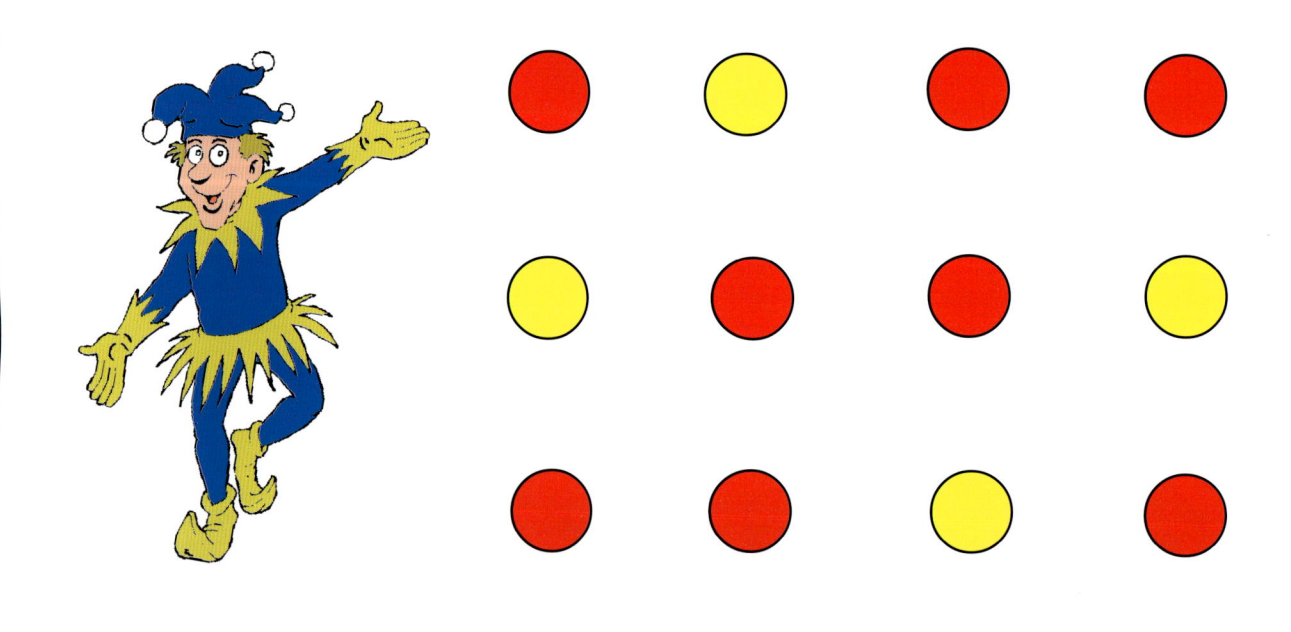

Mind Building Math

Grouping Objects

This picture shows the number and color of toy cars that are sold in one box.

How many boxes will the rest of the cars fill? _____
Circle groups of four cars to help you find the answer.

© 2004 The Critical Thinking Company • www.CriticalThinking.com • 800-458-4849

Grouping Objects — Mind Building Math

1. How many buttons are on this shirt? _____

2. How many more shirts can be made using the buttons below? _____

3. Will any buttons be left over? _____
   How many? _____

4. How many buttons are needed to complete the shirts below so each shirt has 3 buttons? _____

Mind Building Math | Grouping Objects

1. How many bikes like this can be made from the wheels below? ____

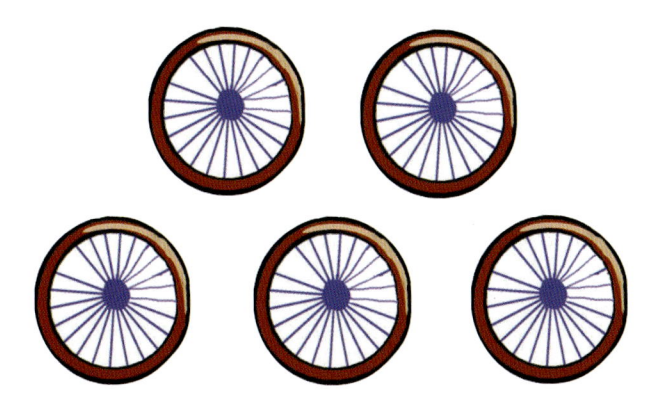

2. Will any wheels be left over? _____
   How many? _____

3. How many wheels are needed to finish these four bikes? _____

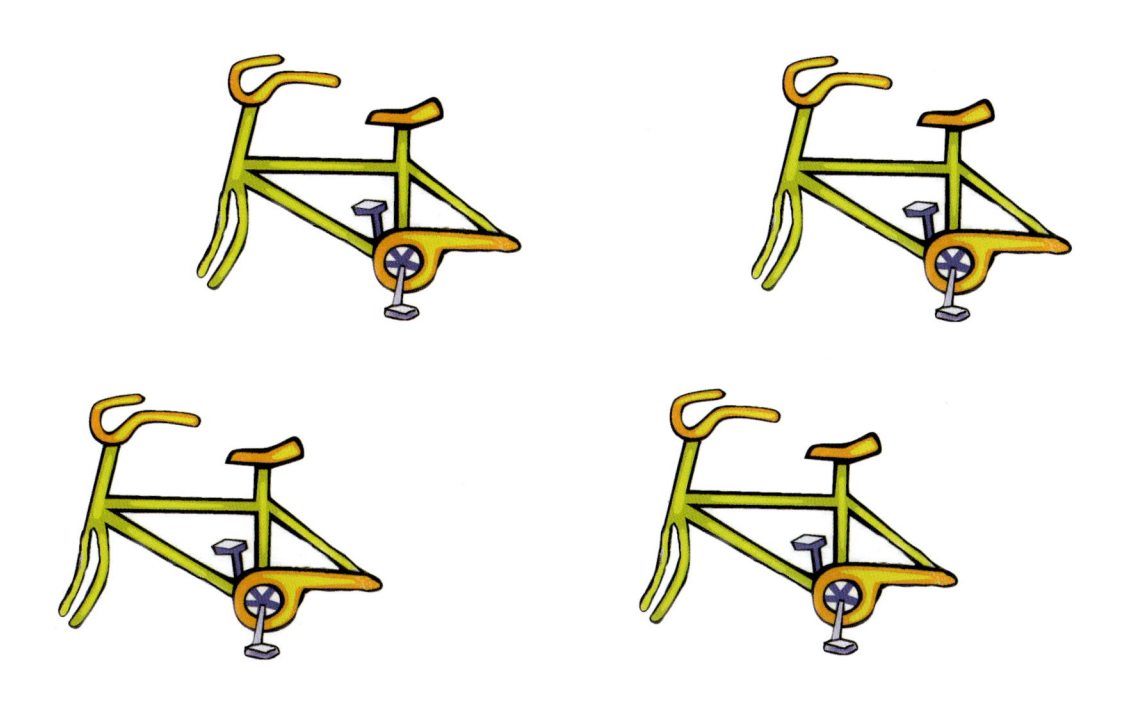

Grouping Objects Mind Building Math

A basket holds 10 strawberries.

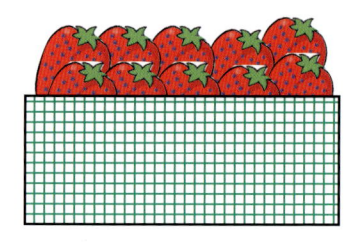

1. How many baskets will these strawberries fill? _____

2. How many strawberries are left over? _____

4. How many baskets will these strawberries fill? _____

5. How many strawberries are left over? _____

Mind Building Math

Grouping Objects

Little Dragon will pick only the apples that look like the one he is holding. Count only those apples on the trees.

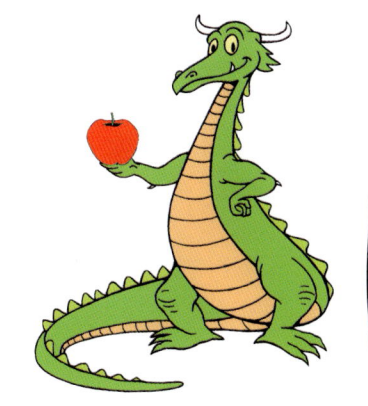

1. How many apples will he pick? _____

One basket holds 10 apples.

2. How many baskets will Little Dragon fill with the apples he picked? _____
Count by 10s to help find the answer.

Adding   Mind Building Math

Dave's birthday cake looks like this.

1a. How old is Dave? _____

1b. How old will he be on his next birthday? _____

_____

Today is Maria's birthday. Last year her birthday cake looked like this.

2a. How old was Maria last year? _____

2b. How old is she this year? _____

2c. How old will she be next year? _____

Mind Building Math

Adding

This is Braden on his birthday three years ago.

1. How old was he then? _____

2. How old is Braden now? _____

3. Draw the candles on his cake below.

Adding   Mind Building Math

Draw a line from each card on the left to one card on the right to make a pair that adds up to 10.

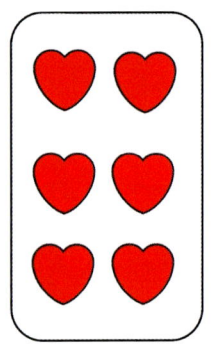

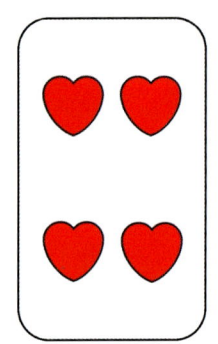

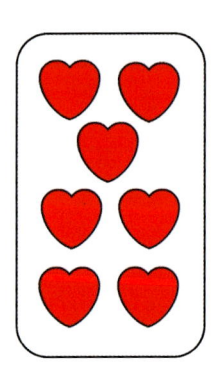

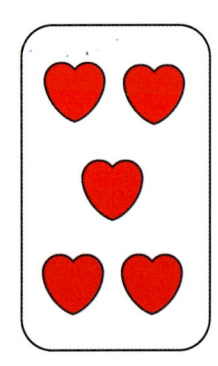

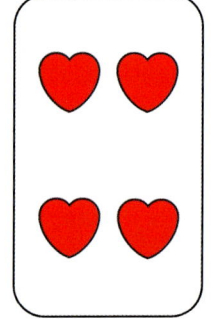

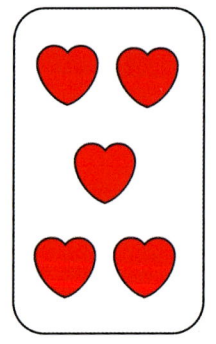

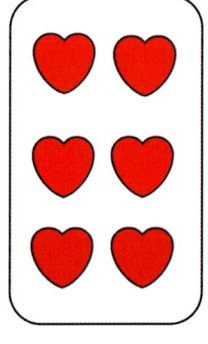

Mind Building Math

Adding

In each set, circle the 2 small squares whose dots *or* numbers add up to 10.

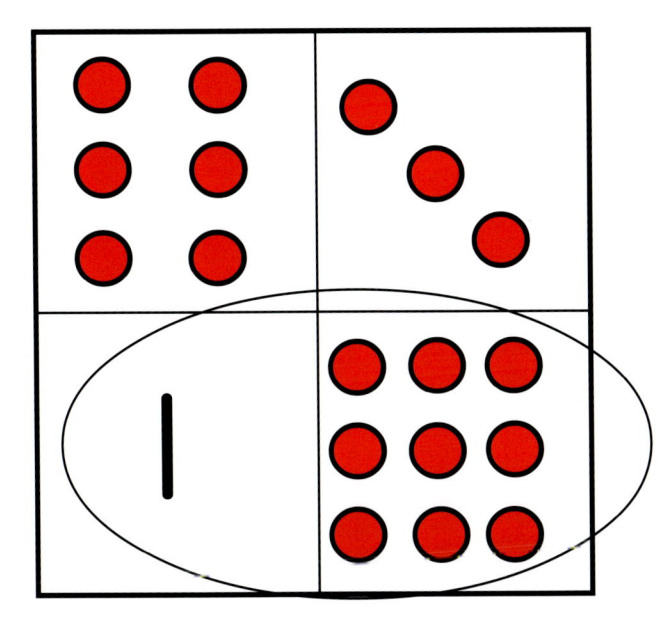

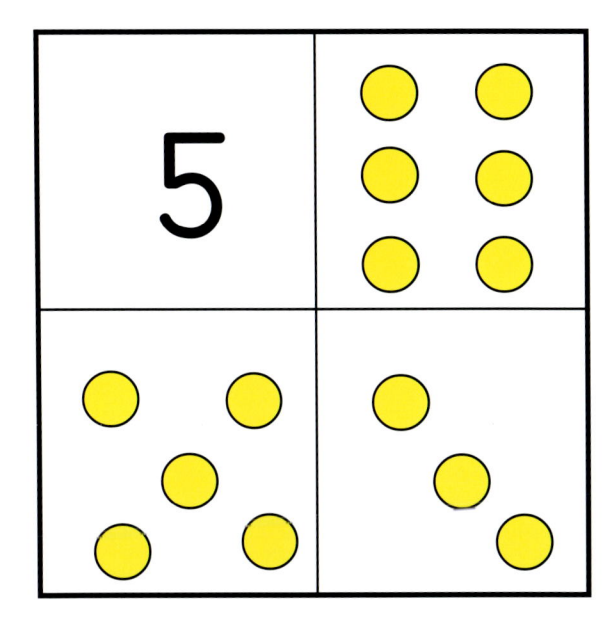

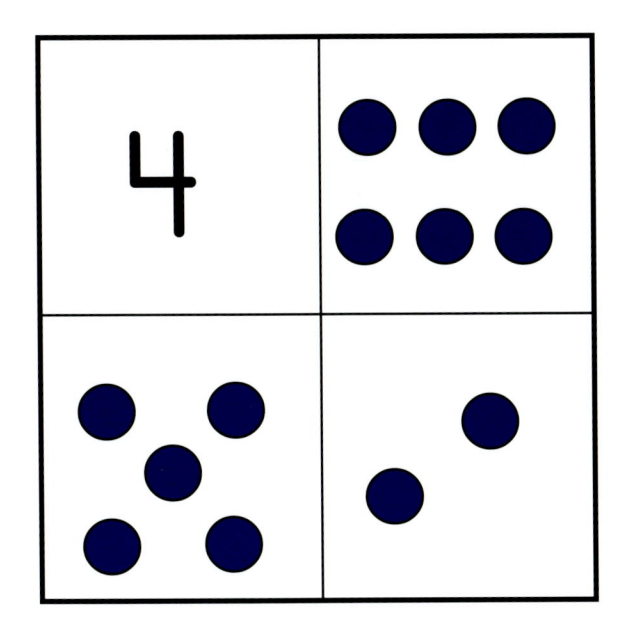

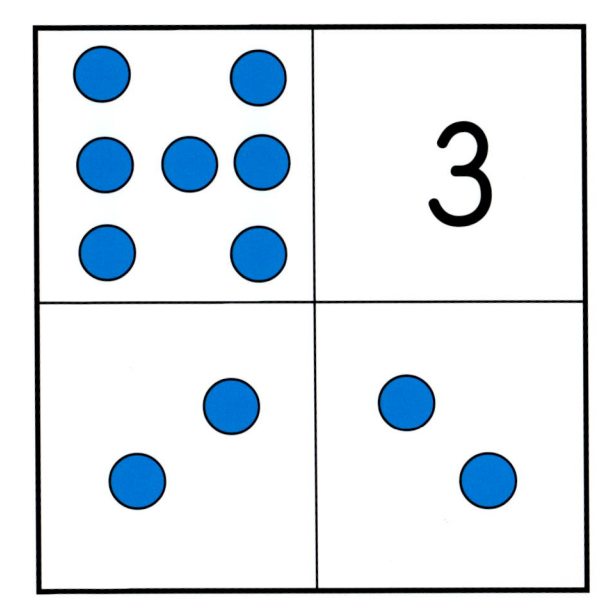

Adding Mind Building Math

In each set, circle the 2 small squares whose dots add up to 10.

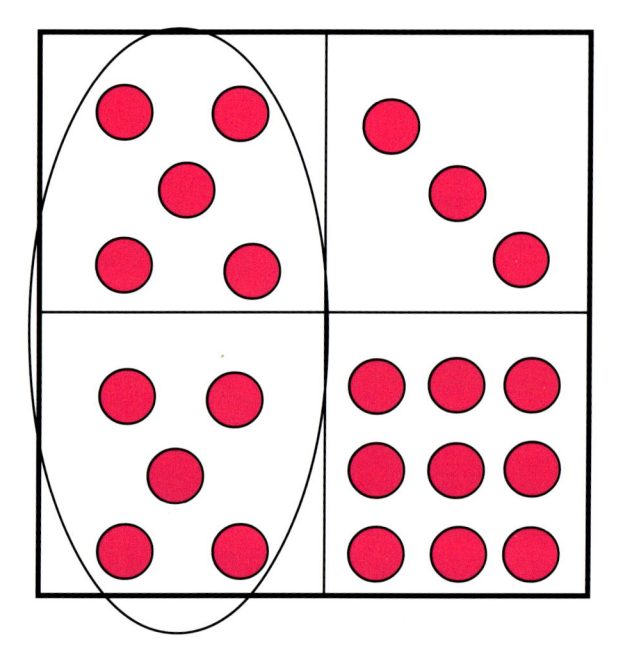

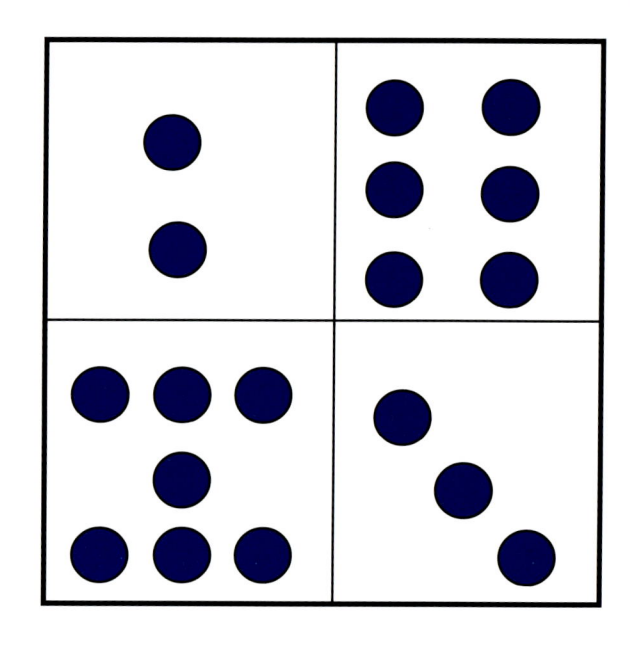

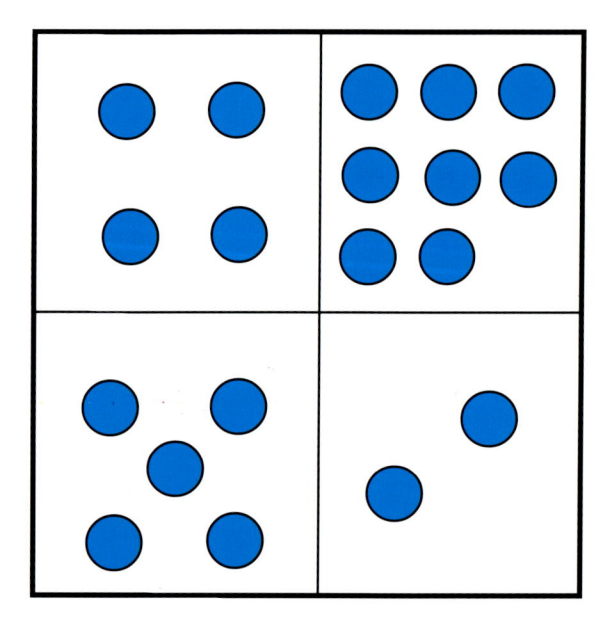

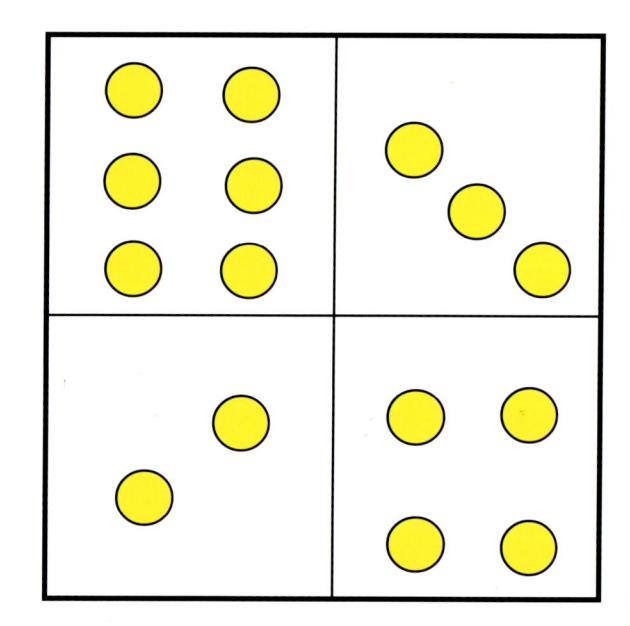

Mind Building Math Adding

There were 10 beads on each necklace before some fell off. Count how many beads are left on each necklace, and draw circles on each necklace to make 10 again.

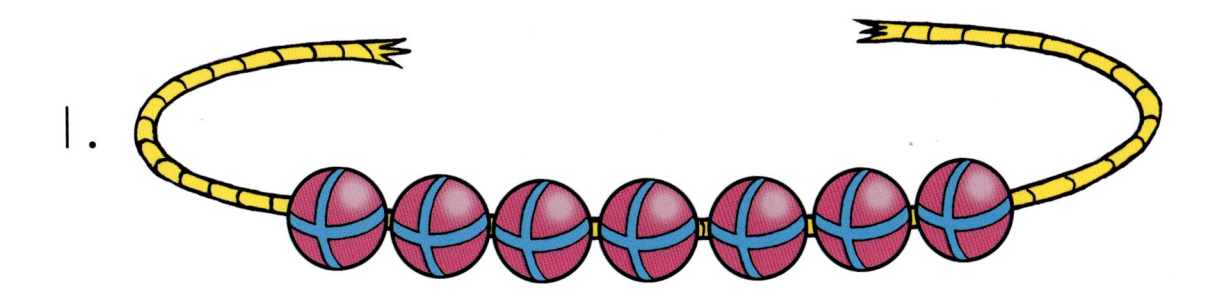

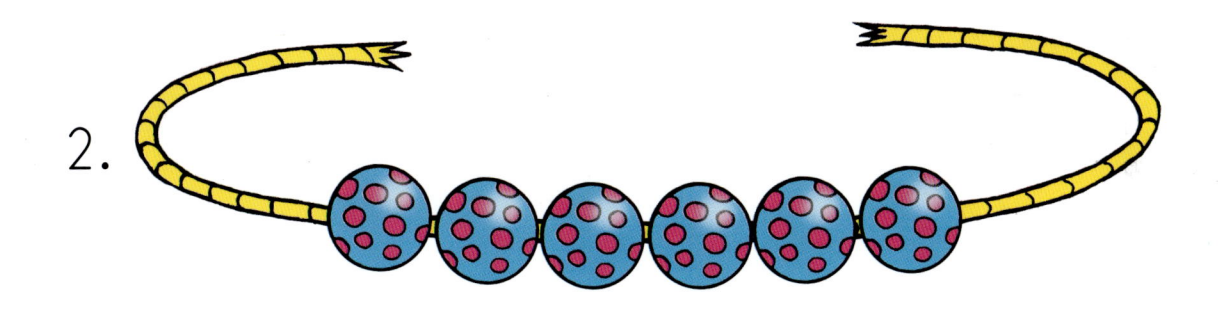

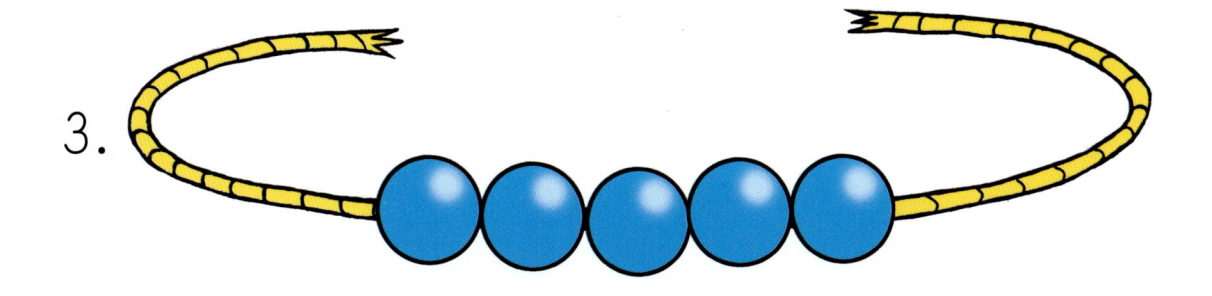

1.

2.

3.

Adding Mind Building Math

Lots of bugs came to the picnic.
Count how many of each kind.
Write how many of each kind on the line.

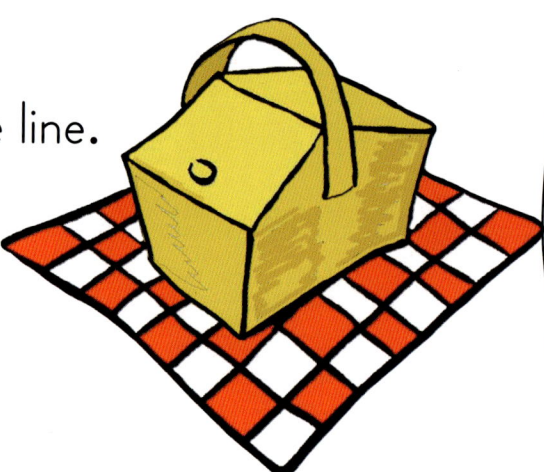

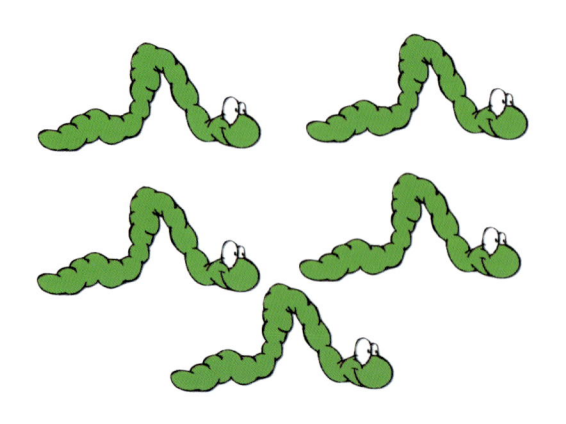

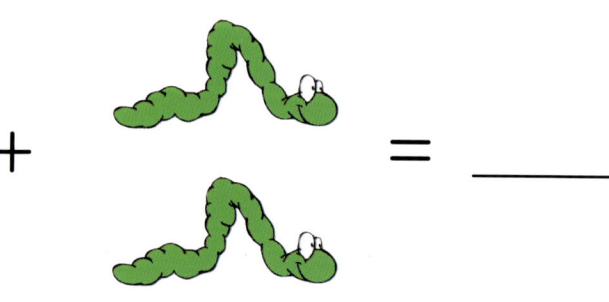

3 + 2 = ___

4 + 3 = ___

5 + 2 = ___

52   © 2004 The Critical Thinking Company • www.CriticalThinking.com • 800-458-4849

Mind Building Math — Adding

It takes ten rings on the post to win a prize. Some rings have already been tossed. Draw the missing rings needed to win a prize. Write the number of missing rings in the number sentence.

1. 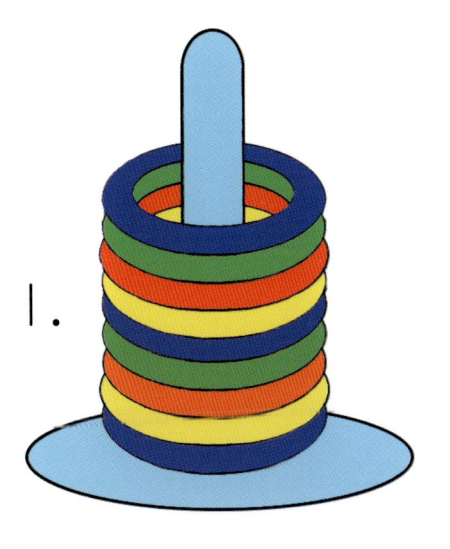 9 + ____ = 10

2. 7 + ____ = 10

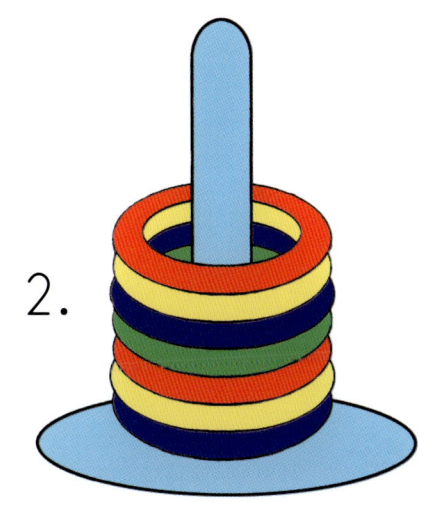

3. 4 + ____ = 10

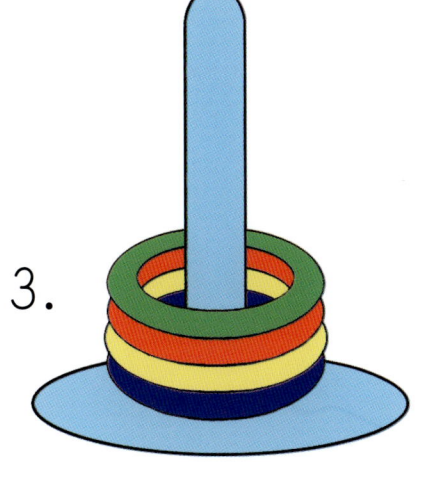

Adding   Mind Building Math

1. Six flowers are growing in this flower box. Three flowers are red, and the other flowers are white. How many flowers are white? _____ Color the flowers to help find the answer. Complete the number sentence.

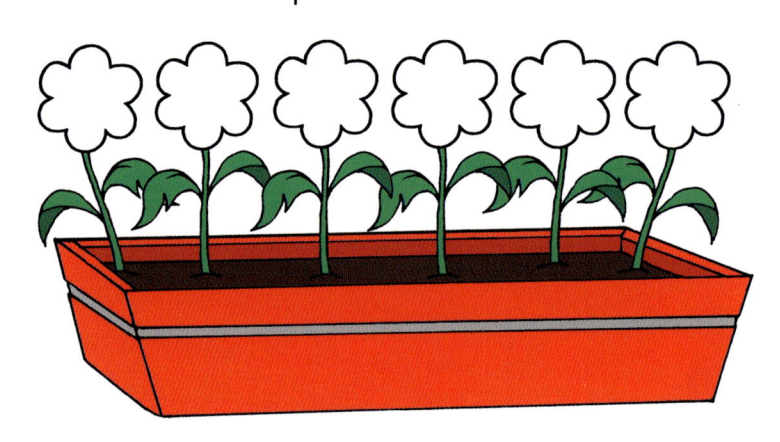

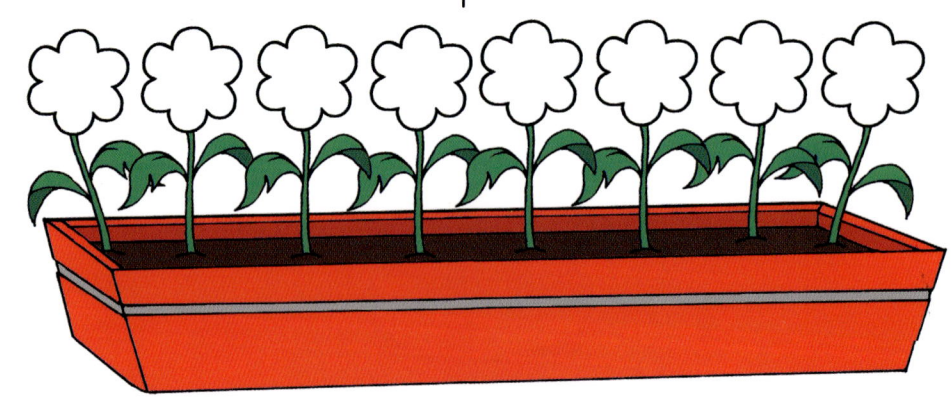

_____ + _____ = __6__

2. Eight flowers are growing in this flower box. Five flowers are red, and the other flowers are white. How many flowers are white? _____ Color the flowers to help find the answer. Complete the number sentence.

_____ + _____ = __8__

Mind Building Math

Adding

1. Little Dragon has 8 apples. Six apples are red and the other apples are white. How many apples are white? _____
Color the apples to help find the answer.
Complete the number sentence.

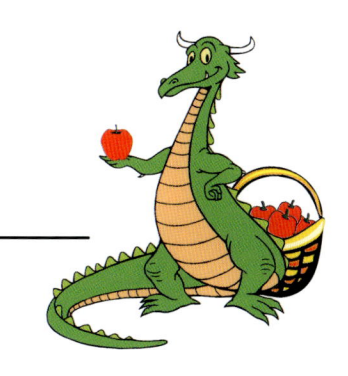

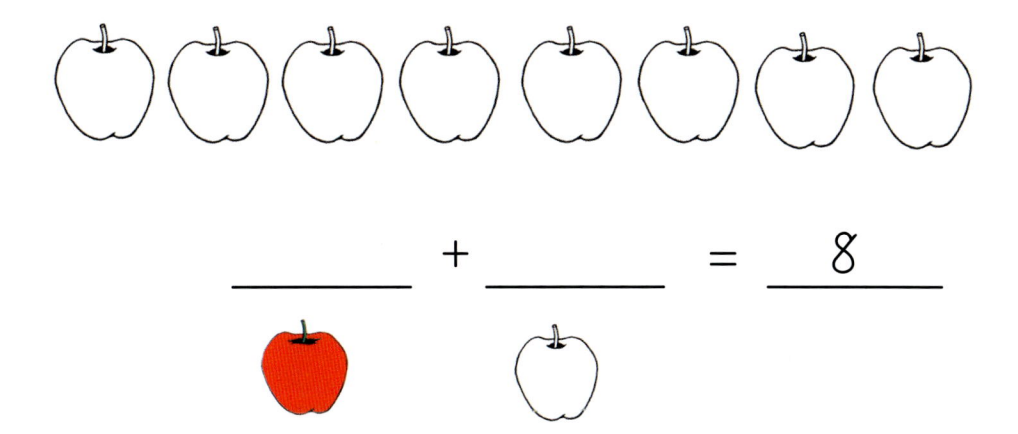

_____ + _____ = __8__

2. Grandma has 10 apples. Seven apples are red and the other apples are white. How many apples are white? _____
Color the apples to help find the answer.
Complete the number sentence.

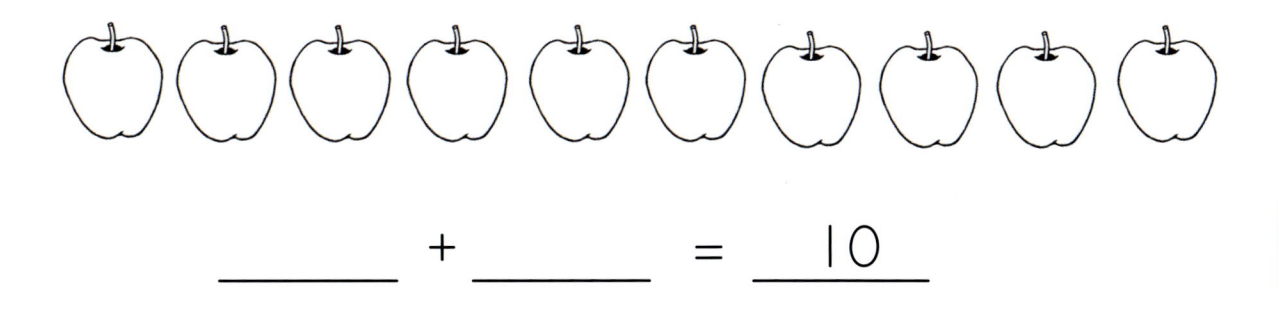

_____ + _____ = __10__

© 2004 The Critical Thinking Company • www.CriticalThinking.com • 800-458-4849

55

Adding

Mind Building Math

In each box, draw the number of balls needed to make the total number of balls on the right.

1. ●●● + ☐ = ●●● ●●●

2. 🟡🟡 🟡🟡🟡 + ☐ = 🟡🟡🟡🟡🟡 🟡🟡🟡🟡🟡

3. ●● ●● + ☐ = ●●●●● ●●●●●

4. 🟢🟢🟢 🟢🟢 + ☐ = 🟢🟢🟢🟢 🟢🟢🟢🟢🟢

Mind Building Math   Adding

At the school fair, each fish is worth the points marked on it. You earn points for each fish you catch.

1. How many points is this fish worth? _____

2. How many points will you earn if you catch both these fish? _____

3. How many points will you earn if you catch both these fish? _____

4. Circle two fish that are worth 10 points together.

Adding   Mind Building Math

In this bean bag toss game, each kind of fruit is worth the points marked on it.

6 (apple)	3 (orange)	4 (lemon)
2 (strawberry)	7 (banana)	5 (pear)

1. How many points is the apple worth? _____

2. How many points are the apple and strawberry worth together? _____

3. How many points are the lemon and orange worth together? _____

4. Circle two pieces of fruit that together are worth 10 points.

5. Put an X on two other pieces of fruit that together are worth 10 points.

58   © 2004 The Critical Thinking Company • www.CriticalThinking.com • 800-458-4849

Mind Building Math

Subtracting

Eight bunnies were playing hide and seek with their mother. The mother found 1 bunny behind a flower box and the 2 bunnies behind bushes.

1. How many bunnies did the mother find? _____

2. How many bunnies were still hiding? _____

3. How many bunnies were still hiding behind flower boxes? _____

© 2004 The Critical Thinking Company • www.CriticalThinking.com • 800-458-4849

Subtracting   Mind Building Math

1. At the library, Juanita wants to find 10 books about cats. Look at the books she found so far.

    How many more books does she need to find? _____

    CATS & KITTENS
    WILD CATS
    CARING FOR CATS
    BIG BOOK OF CATS
    ALL KINDS OF CATS

2. Mike is carrying his new books. He has read 3 of these books.

    How many books does he still have to read? _____

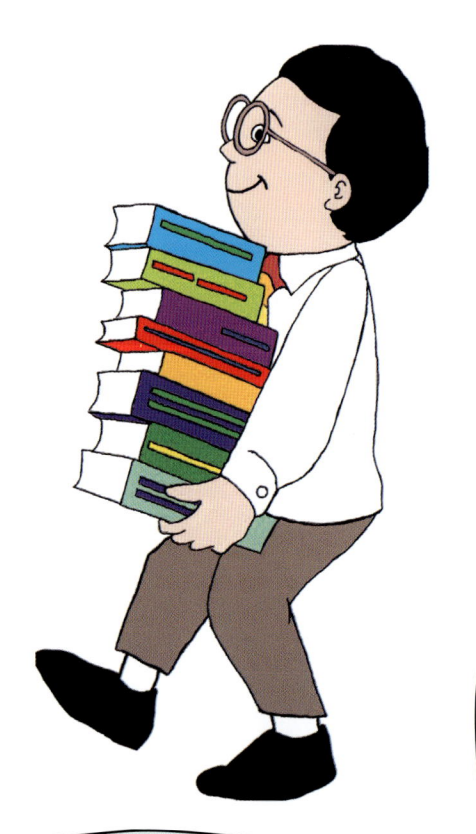

Mind Building Math

Adding/Subtracting

1. Count the number of balls Red Rob is juggling. Count the number of balls Blue Ben is juggling. Complete the number sentence.

   ____ + ____ = ____
   RR   BB

2. If Red Rob adds 2 balls, how many will he have in all?

   ____ + __2__ = ____

3. If Blue Ben drops one ball, how many balls will he have left? Complete the number sentence.

   ____ − __1__ = ____

Subtracting — Mind Building Math

1. There were this many pennies inside my bank.

   I took this many out.

   How many are still inside the bank? _____

2. There were this many sticks of gum inside the package.

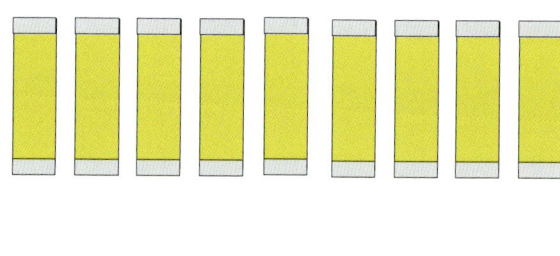

   I took this many out.

   How many are still inside the package? _____

Mind Building Math

Subtracting

Ann and Ben bought these cookies at the bake sale.

1. How many did they buy? _____

Ann ate these cookies

Ben ate these cookies.

2. In the row at the top, cross off the cookies Ann and Ben ate. How many cookies were left? _____

3. Who ate more cookies?   Ben   or   Ann

© 2004 The Critical Thinking Company • www.CriticalThinking.com • 800-458-4849

Subtracting   Mind Building Math

1. Terry is having a lemonade sale.
   Count how many cups she wants to sell today. _____

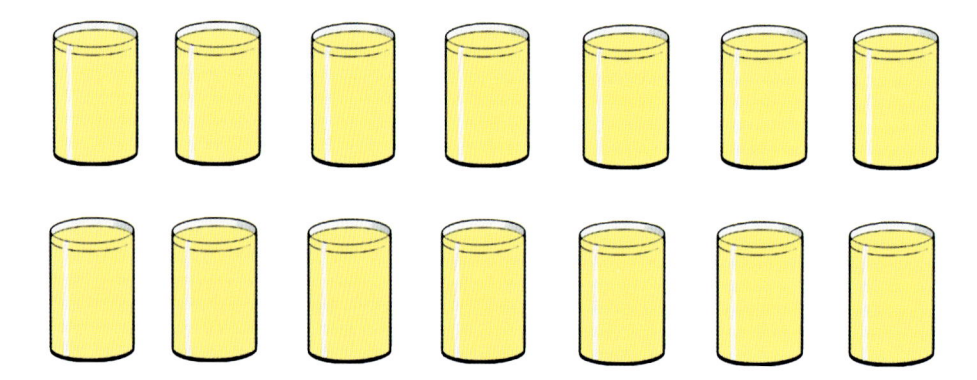

2. At the end of the day, Terry had not sold the cups shown below. How many cups were not sold? _____

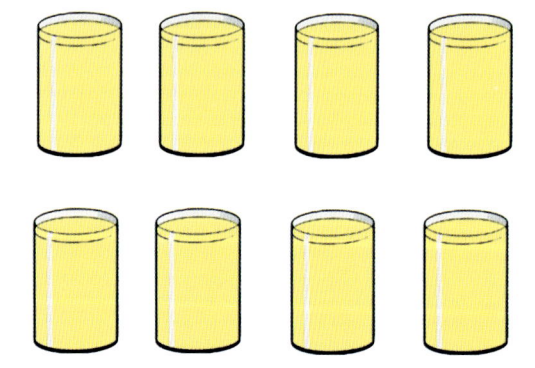

3. In the picture at the top, circle the cups that were not sold. How many did Terry sell? _____

Mind Building Math

Subtracting

1. There were this many pennies inside my piggy bank.

   I took 3 pennies out. How many are left inside the bank? _____

2. There were this many pennies inside my piggy bank.

   I took 5 pennies out. How many are left inside the bank? _____

Subtracting

Mind Building Math

Dad made 15 pancakes.
Draw the pancakes below.

Jan ate 3. Mom ate 4. Dad ate 6.
Put an X on each pancake they ate.

1. How many pancakes did they eat in all? _____

2. How many were left? _____

Mind Building Math

Subtracting

Jon was served 20 peas. Draw the peas on the plate.

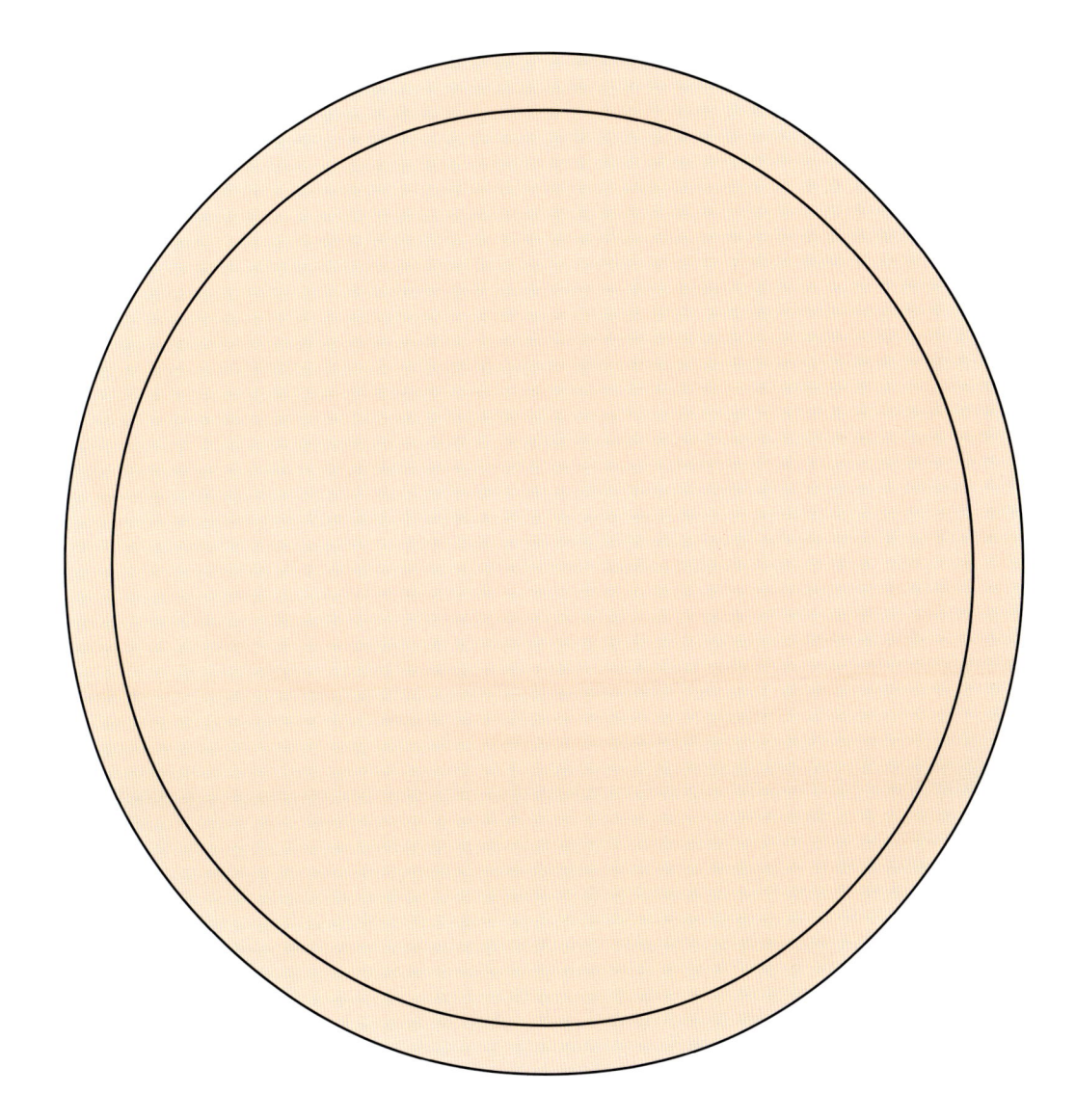

He ate 10 of them. Put an X on each pea he ate.

How many are left? _____

Subtracting   Mind Building Math

1. How many pieces are in this pizza? _____

2. Ann ate 3 pieces. Write an A on her pieces.
   Bobby ate 2 pieces. Write a B on his pieces.
   Clare ate 1 piece. Write a C on her piece.

3. How many pieces were left for Dave? _____

4. Circle the name of the person who ate the most pieces.

   Dave   Bobby   Ann   Clare

Kate brought 15 treats to the party.
There were this many cupcakes and the rest were cookies.

1. How many cupcakes did Kate bring? _____

2. Draw how many cookies she brought to the party.

Fractions Whole/Half

Mind Building Math

Draw a line to cut each food into two parts that are about equal.

Mind Building Math

Fractions Whole/Half

Draw a line to cut each shape into two equal parts.

Fractions Whole/Half

Mind Building Math

Steven likes to share by giving away half of each type of food in his lunchbox. Circle how much of each kind of food Steven will give to his friends.

72 © 2004 The Critical Thinking Company • www.CriticalThinking.com • 800-458-4849

Mind Building Math   **Fractions Whole/Half**

Two brothers decided to share their cookies with their little sister. They divided all the cookies they found in one package. Some cookies were broken.

1. The oldest brother, Jared, took only the cookies that were whole. Circle Jared's cookies. How many whole cookies did he take? _____

2. The little sister, Ali, took all the cookies that were broken in half. Put an X on Ali's cookies. How many half cookies did she take? _____

3. The younger brother, Steven, took the cookies that were not whole but were bigger than half. How many cookies did he take? _____

Fractions Whole/Half

Mind Building Math

Three kids divided a bag of apples. Some of the apples were whole. Some of the apples had been cut.

1. Jen took only the apples that were whole. Circle Jen's apples.
   How many whole apples did Jen take? _____

2. Sam took the apples that were cut in half. Put an X on Sam's apples.
   How many half apples did Sam take? _____

3. Raul agreed to take the apples that were not whole, but were bigger than half.
   How many apple pieces did Raul take? _____

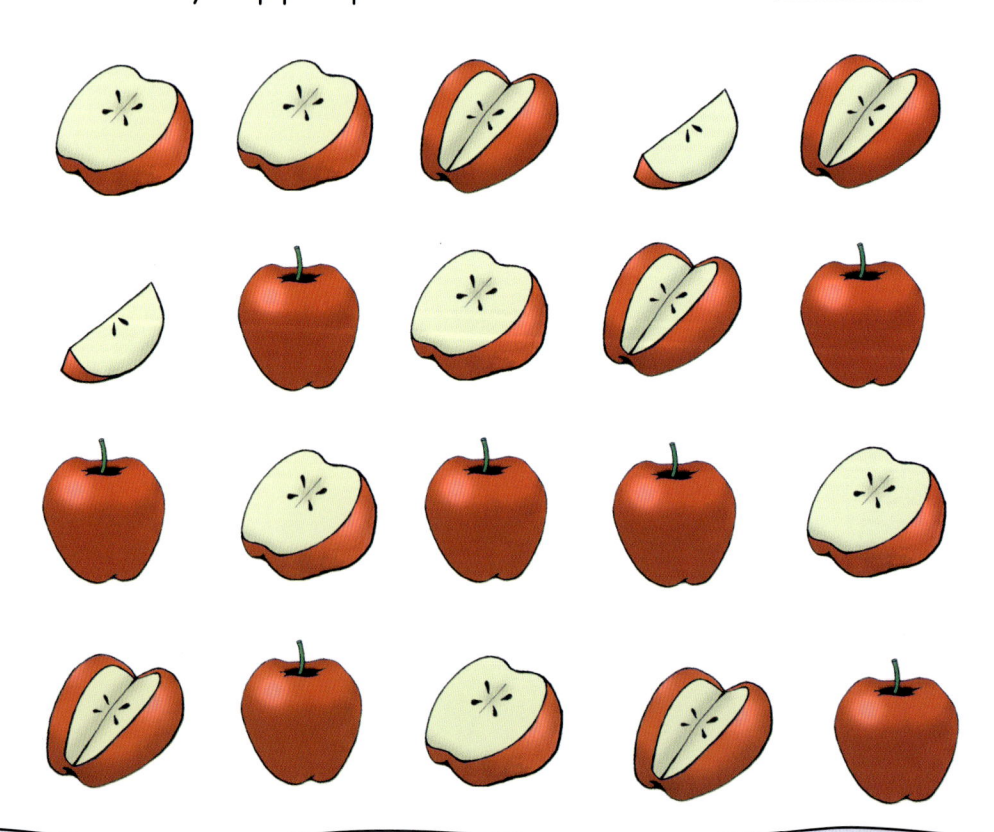

74 © 2004 The Critical Thinking Company • www.CriticalThinking.com • 800-458-4849

Mind Building Math

Counting by 10s

Help the cat cross the river. Draw a path from 10 to 100 counting by tens.

Counting by 10s

Mind Building Math

Help Dina Dinosaur find her eggs. Draw a path to connect the footprints in the correct order counting by tens.

Mind Building Math

Counting by 5s

Help Danny Dinosaur get back to his family. Draw a path to connect the footprints in the correct order counting by fives.

5, 10, 15, 20, 25, 30, 35, 40, 45, 50

© 2004 The Critical Thinking Company • www.CriticalThinking.com • 800-458-4849

77

Counting by 10s

Mind Building Math

Count by tens. In each row, fill in the missing number.

1. 10, 20, ___

2. 40, ___, 60

3. 30, 40, ___

4. ___, 80, 90

Mind Building Math — Counting by 5s

Count by fives. In each row, fill in the missing number.

1. 5, 10, ___

2. 25, ___, 35

3. 15, ___, 25

4. 40, 45, ___

Coin Value — Mind Building Math

1. Which coin would be just enough money to buy an ice cream cone? How much is it worth? _____¢

2. Which coin would be just enough money to buy an ice cream bar? How much is it worth? _____¢

3. Which coin would be just enough money to buy an ice cream sandwich? How much is it worth? _____¢

Mind Building Math

Coin Value

Terry sold strawberries and watermelon at her corner stand.

1. Each giant strawberry cost a nickel.
   Count the strawberries by 5s.
   How much money did she make? _____ ¢

2. Each slice of watermelon cost a nickel.
   Count the slices by 5s.
   How much money did she make? _____ ¢

© 2004 The Critical Thinking Company • www.CriticalThinking.com • 800-458-4849

83

Coin Value   Mind Building Math

Terry sold lemonade and cookies at her corner stand.

1. Each cup of lemonade cost a dime.
   Count the drinks by 10s.
   How much money did she make? _____ ¢

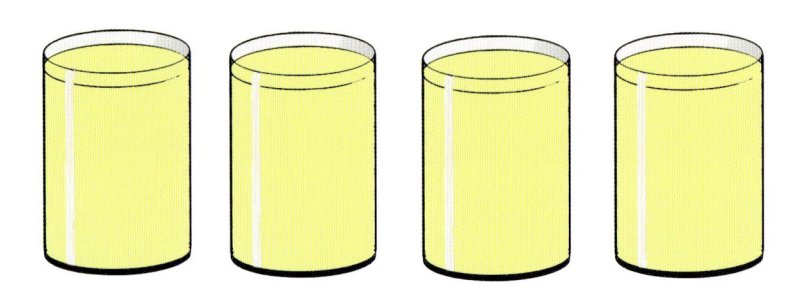

2. Each cookie cost a dime.
   Count the cookies by 10s.
   How much money did she make? _____ ¢

Mind Building Math									Coin Value

CHOCOLATE 10¢

2¢

GUM 5¢

1¢

1. If you have only 5 pennies, can you buy the candy below?

   Yes   No

2. If you have only 7 pennies, can you buy the candy below?

   Yes   No

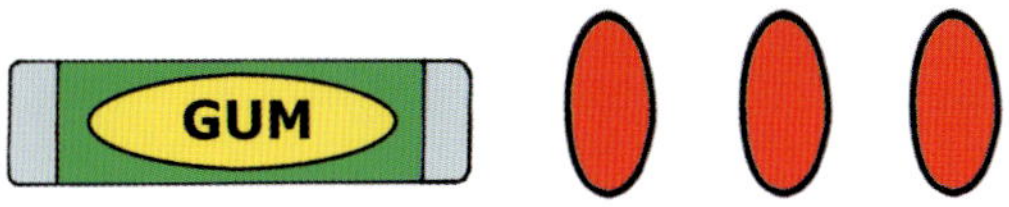

3. If you have only 12 pennies, can you buy the candy below?

   Yes   No

Coin Value   Mind Building Math

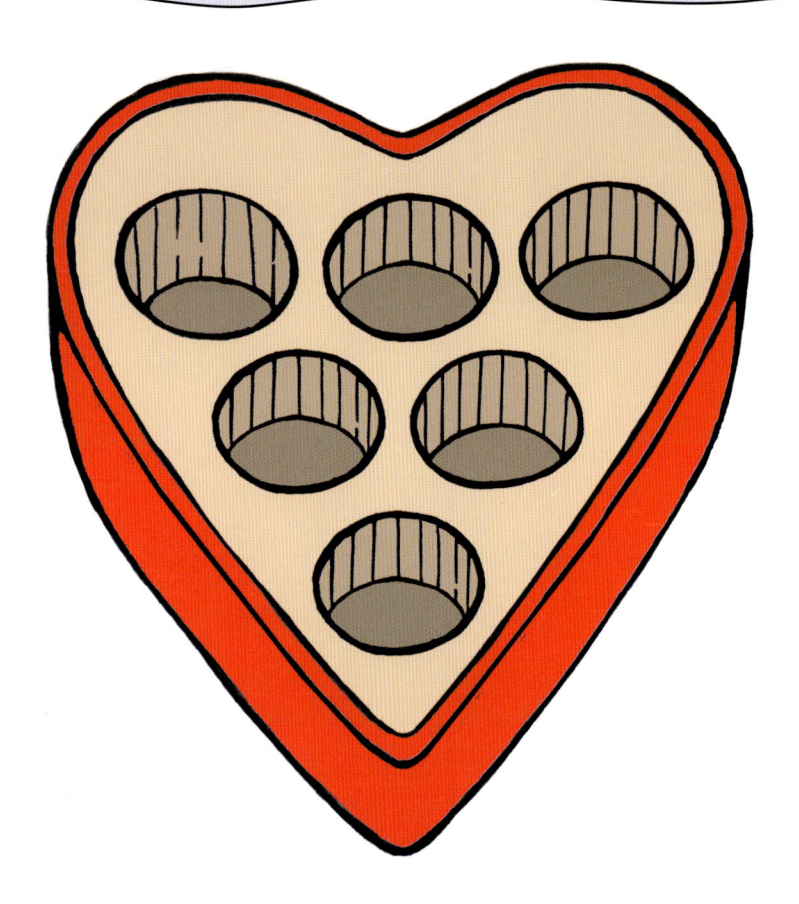

One chocolate costs a penny.

1. How many chocolates will fit in the box? _____

2. How many pennies will 4 chocolates cost? _____

3. How much will one box full of chocolates cost? _____

4. If Kris has 10¢, does she have enough to buy a box of chocolates? _____

Mind Building Math   Extending Patterns

1. Look at the numbers in the first two hoops and think how the numbers are related. Then write the missing numbers in the last hoop.

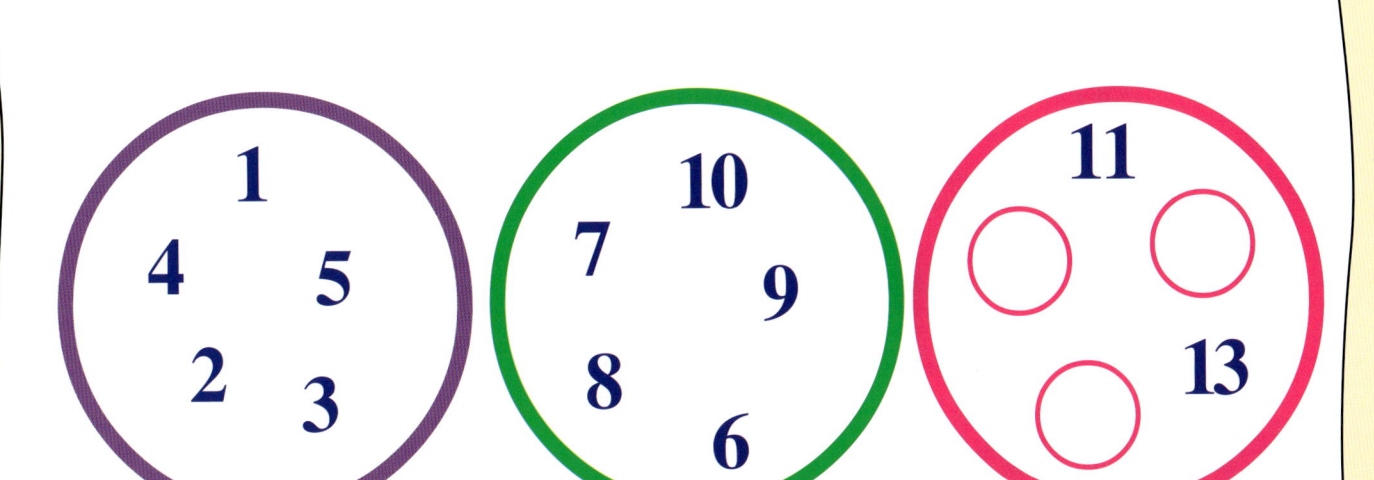

- Purple hoop: 1, 4, 5, 2, 3
- Green hoop: 10, 7, 9, 8, 6
- Pink hoop: 11, ○, ○, ○, 13

2. Write the missing numbers in each hoop.

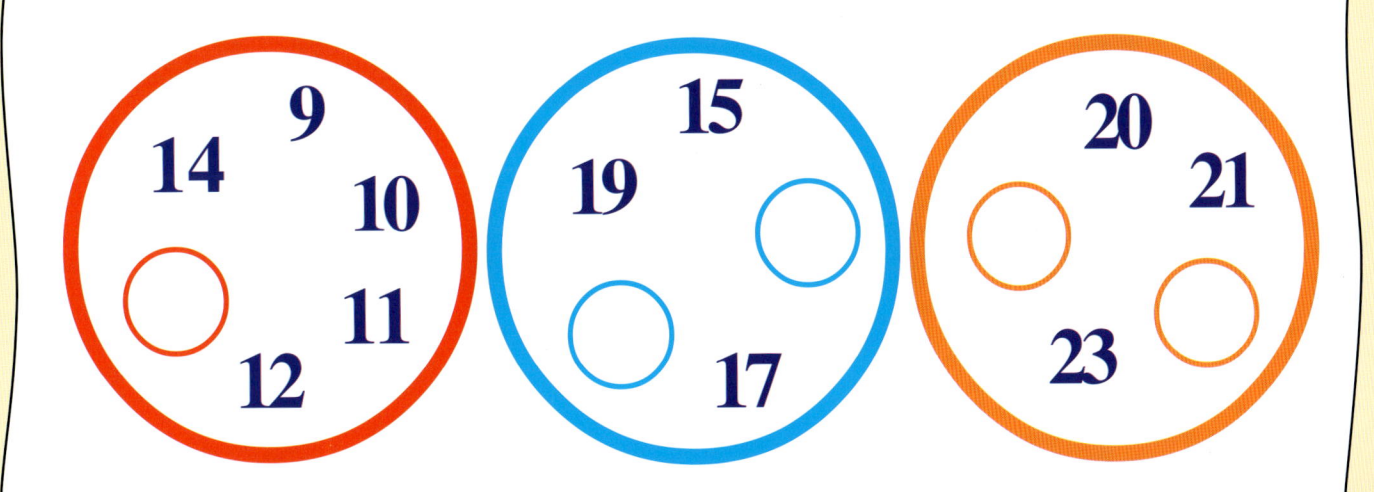

- Red hoop: 9, 14, 10, 11, 12, ○
- Blue hoop: 15, 19, ○, ○, 17
- Orange hoop: 20, 21, ○, ○, 23

87

Extending Patterns   Mind Building Math

The number below each box tells how many objects are in that box. Look for a number pattern to help you figure out how many objects are in the other boxes.

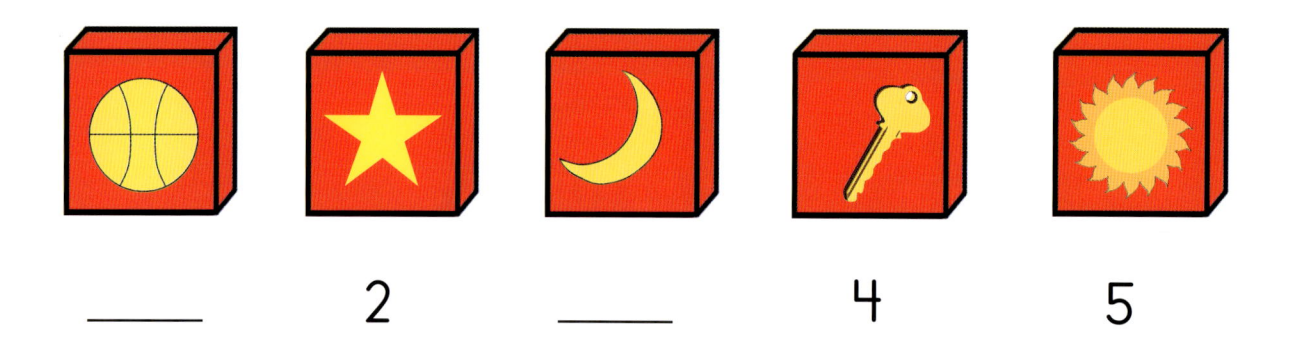

___   2   ___   4   5

1. If there are 2 stars in the star box and 4 keys in the key box, how many moons are in the moon box? ____

2. Circle the box that has two more objects than the star box.

3. How many more suns are there than keys? _____

4. How many balls are in the ball box? _____

Mind Building Math Extending Patterns

1. Describe and then finish the pattern.

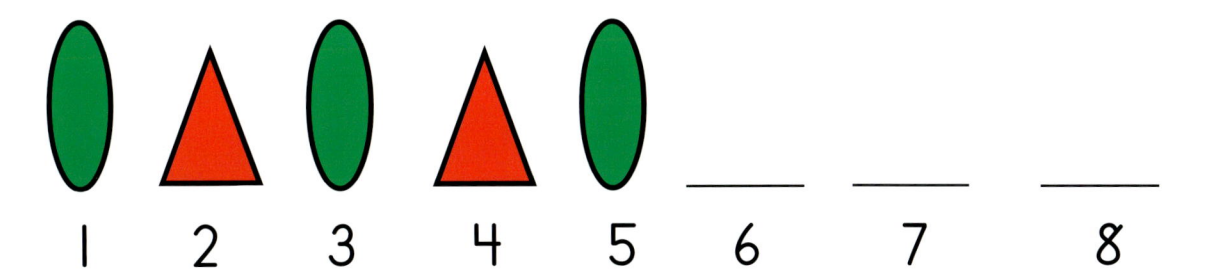

   ⬭ 🔺 ⬭ 🔺 ⬭ ___ ___ ___
   1 2 3 4 5 6   7   8

2. Which shape will be in space 6?   ⬭ or 🔺

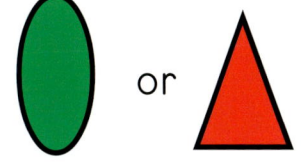

3. Which shape will be in space 8?   ⬭ or 🔺

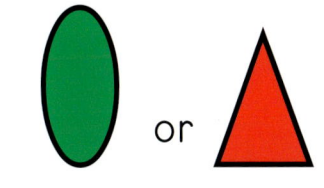

4. Describe and then finish the pattern.

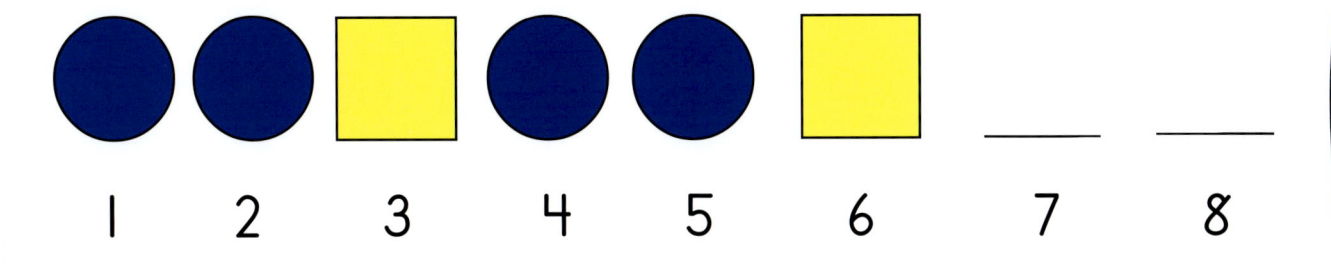

   ● ● ■ ● ● ■ ___ ___
   1 2 3 4 5 6 7   8

5. Which shape will be in space 7?   ● or ■

6. Which shape will be in space 8?   ● or ■

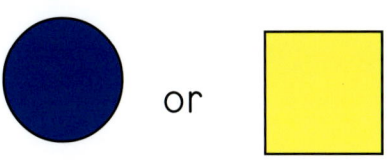

© 2004 The Critical Thinking Company • www.CriticalThinking.com • 800-458-4849

Extending Patterns   Mind Building Math

Clap your hands every time you see hands in the pattern and stomp your foot every time you see a shoe in the pattern.

Clap   Stomp

90
© 2004 The Critical Thinking Company • www.CriticalThinking.com • 800-458-4849

Mind Building Math

Extending Patterns

1. Draw the shapes that come next in this pattern.

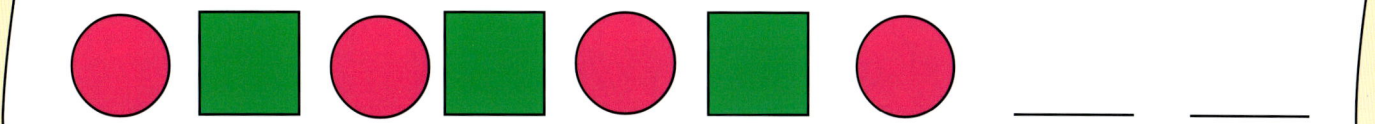

○ ■ ○ ■ ○ ■ ○ ___ ___

2. Draw the shapes that come next in this pattern.

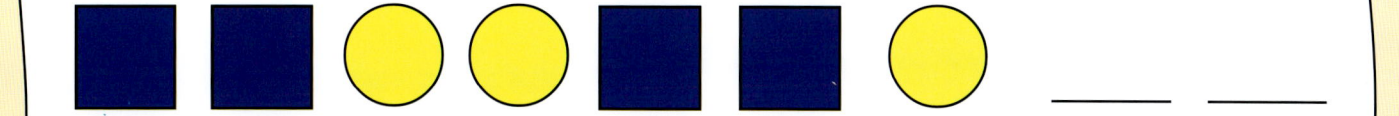

■ ■ ○ ○ ■ ■ ○ ___ ___

3. Draw the shapes that come next in this pattern.

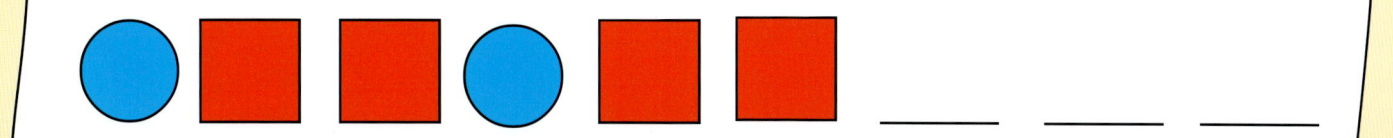

○ ■ ■ ○ ■ ■ ___ ___ ___

© 2004 The Critical Thinking Company • www.CriticalThinking.com • 800-458-4849

Extending Patterns   Mind Building Math

Complete the pattern train. Draw the shapes that come next.

Complete the pattern train. Draw the shapes that come next.

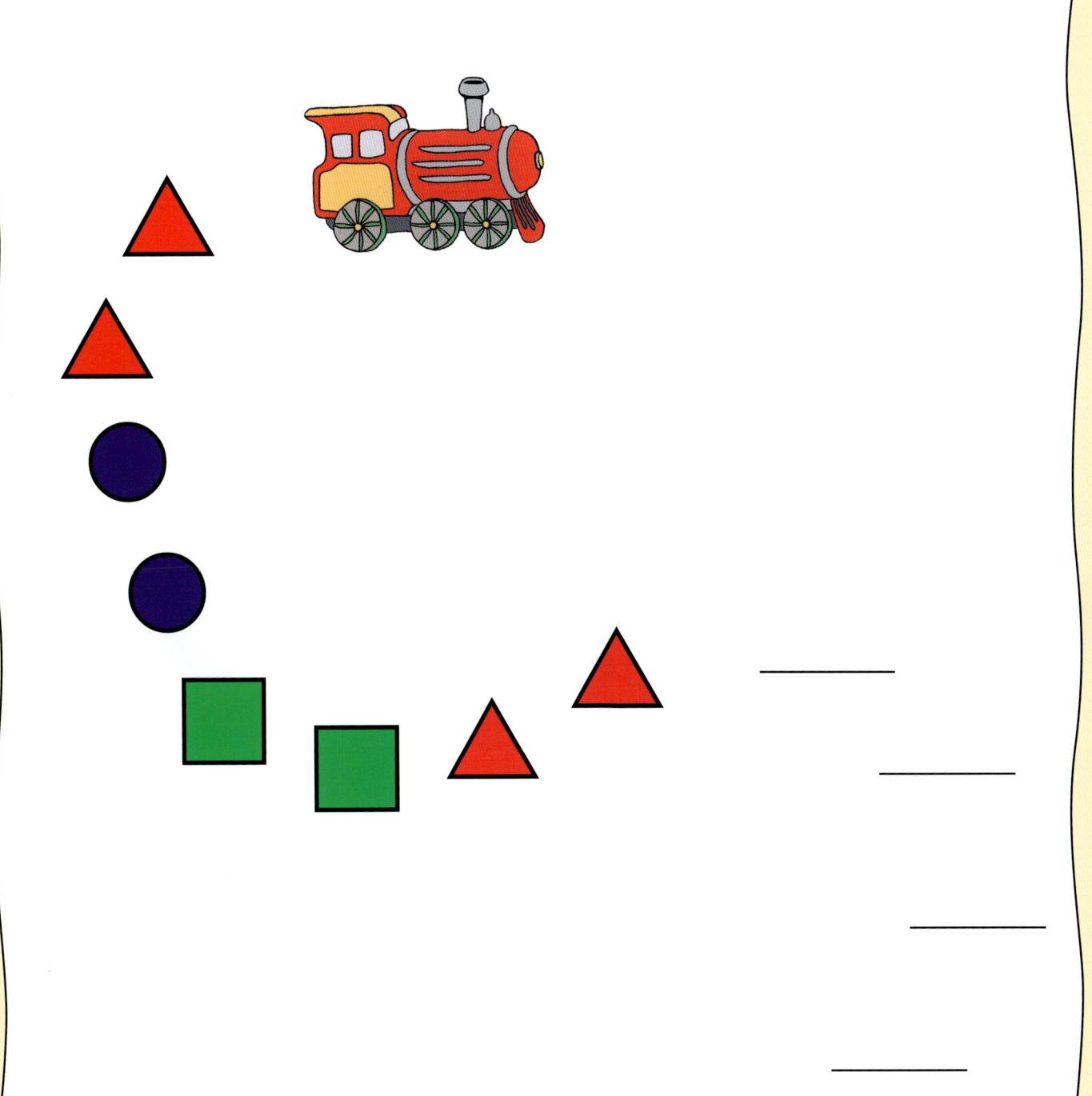

Extending Patterns

Mind Building Math

Draw three figures in each box to continue the pattern.

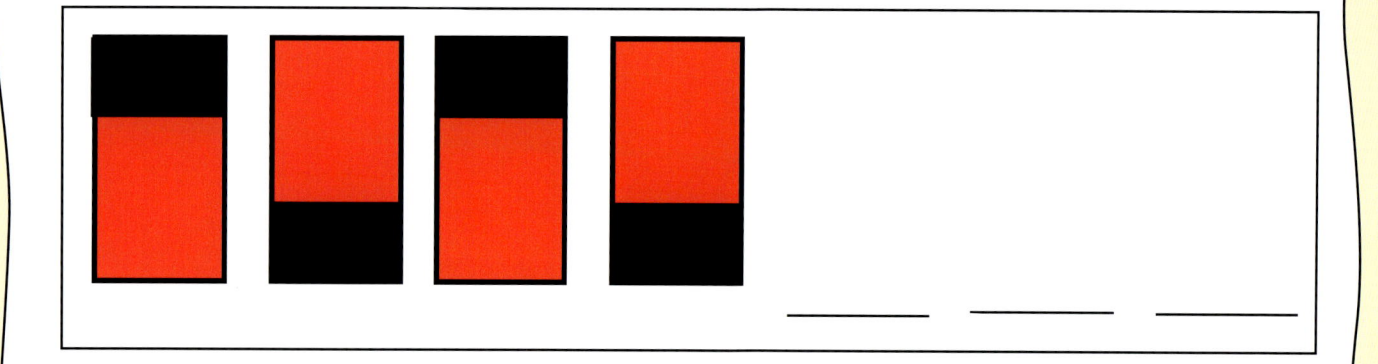

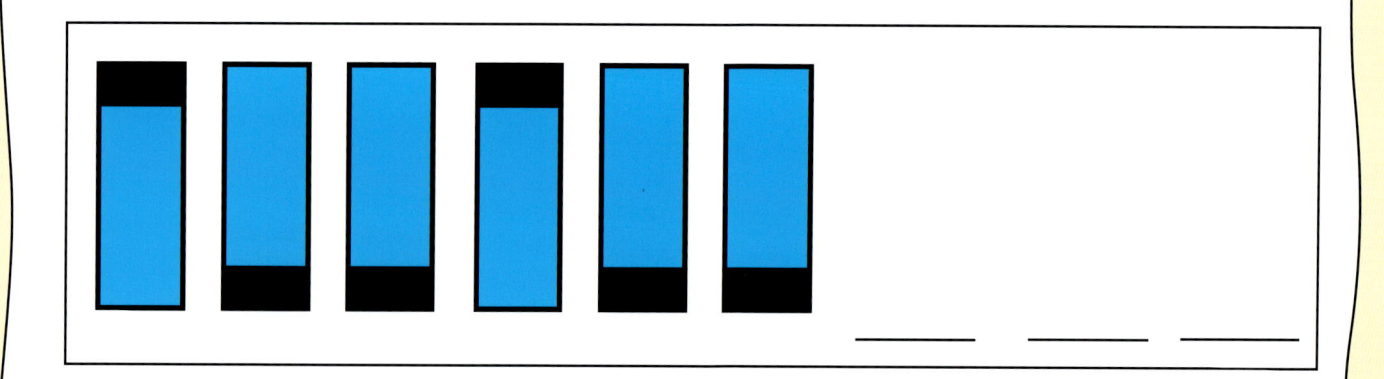

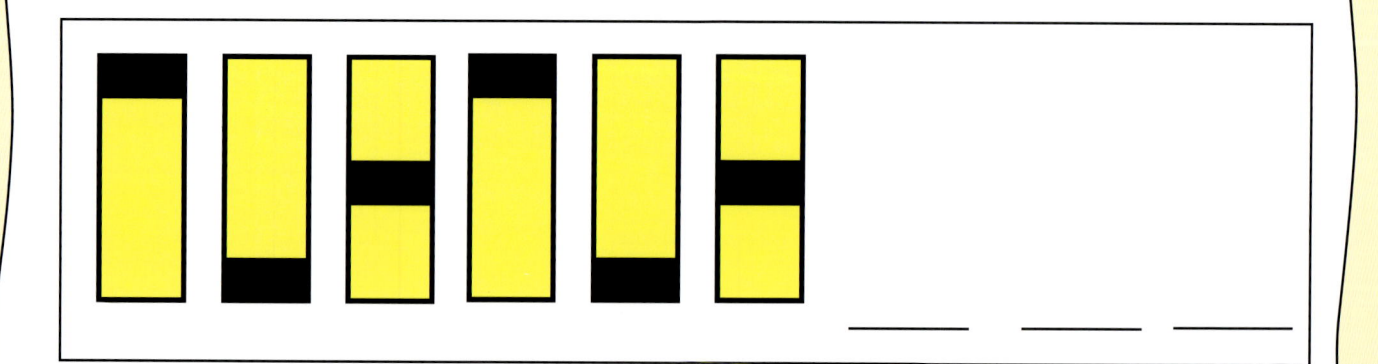

Mind Building Math   Extending Patterns

Draw three figures in each box to continue the pattern.

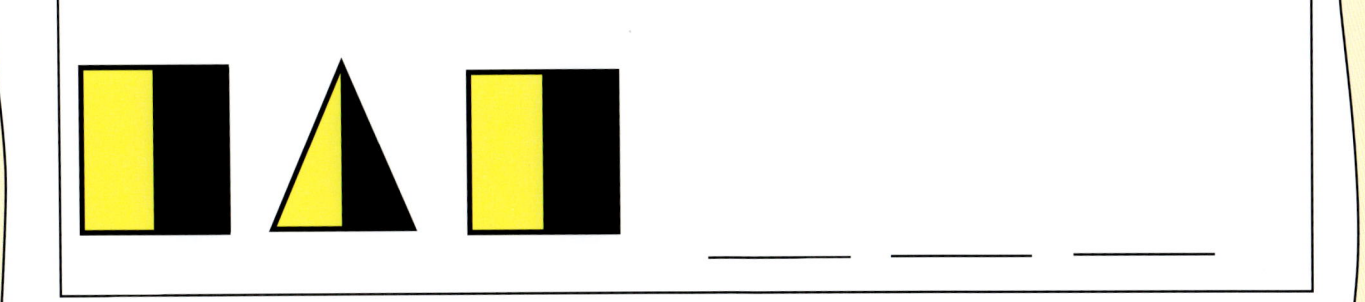

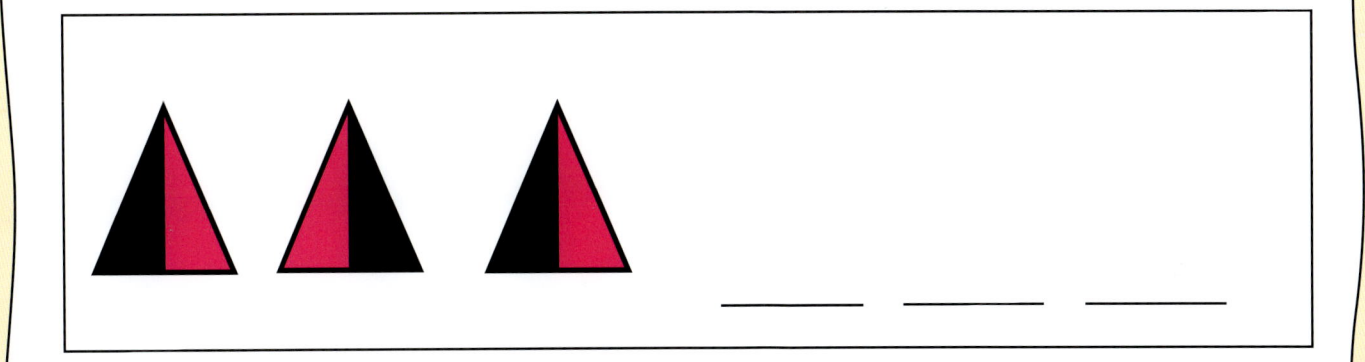

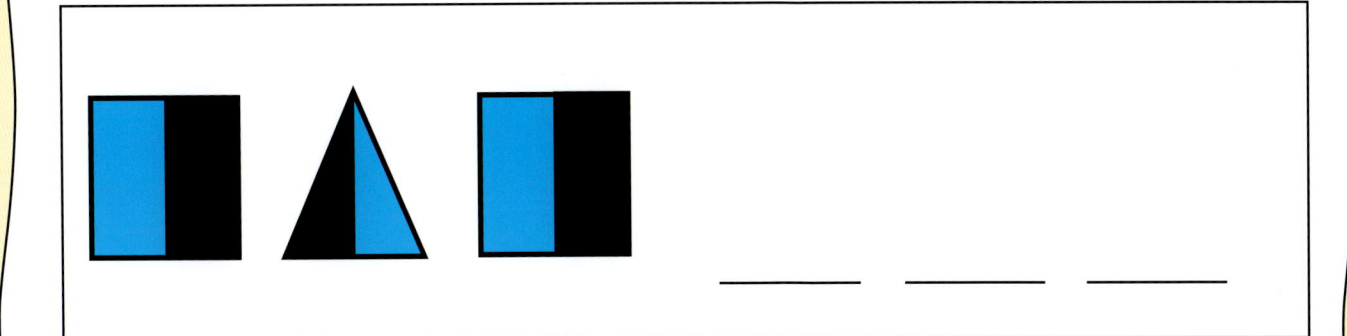

Ordering Objects by Size

Mind Building Math

Circle the smallest yellow star. Draw lines to connect the smallest yellow star to the next biggest yellow star, and so on, until you get to the biggest yellow star.

Mind Building Math

Ordering Objects by Size

Order the balls from smallest to largest. Write a number from 1 to 5 above each ball.

Comparing 2-D Shapes

Mind Building Math

Draw a line to match each sign with its shape.

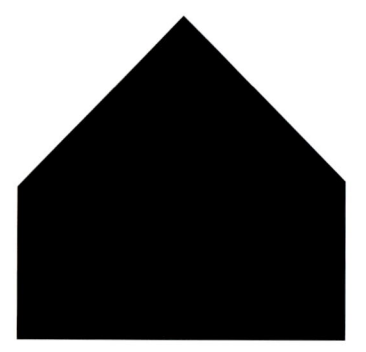

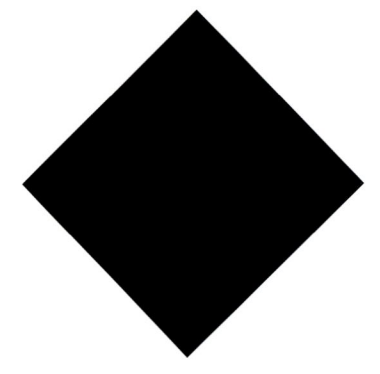

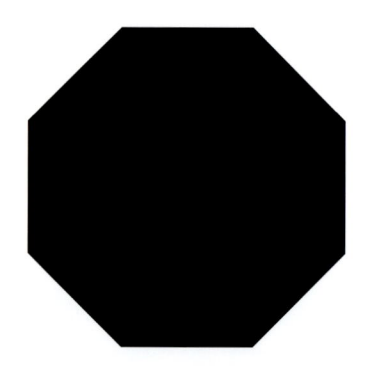

Mind Building Math

Comparing 2-D Shapes

1. Circle all the shapes below that have 3 sides. How many shapes have 3 sides? _____

2. Put an X on all the shapes below that have 4 sides. How many shapes have 4 sides? _____

3. Are there more 3-sided or 4-sided shapes? _____

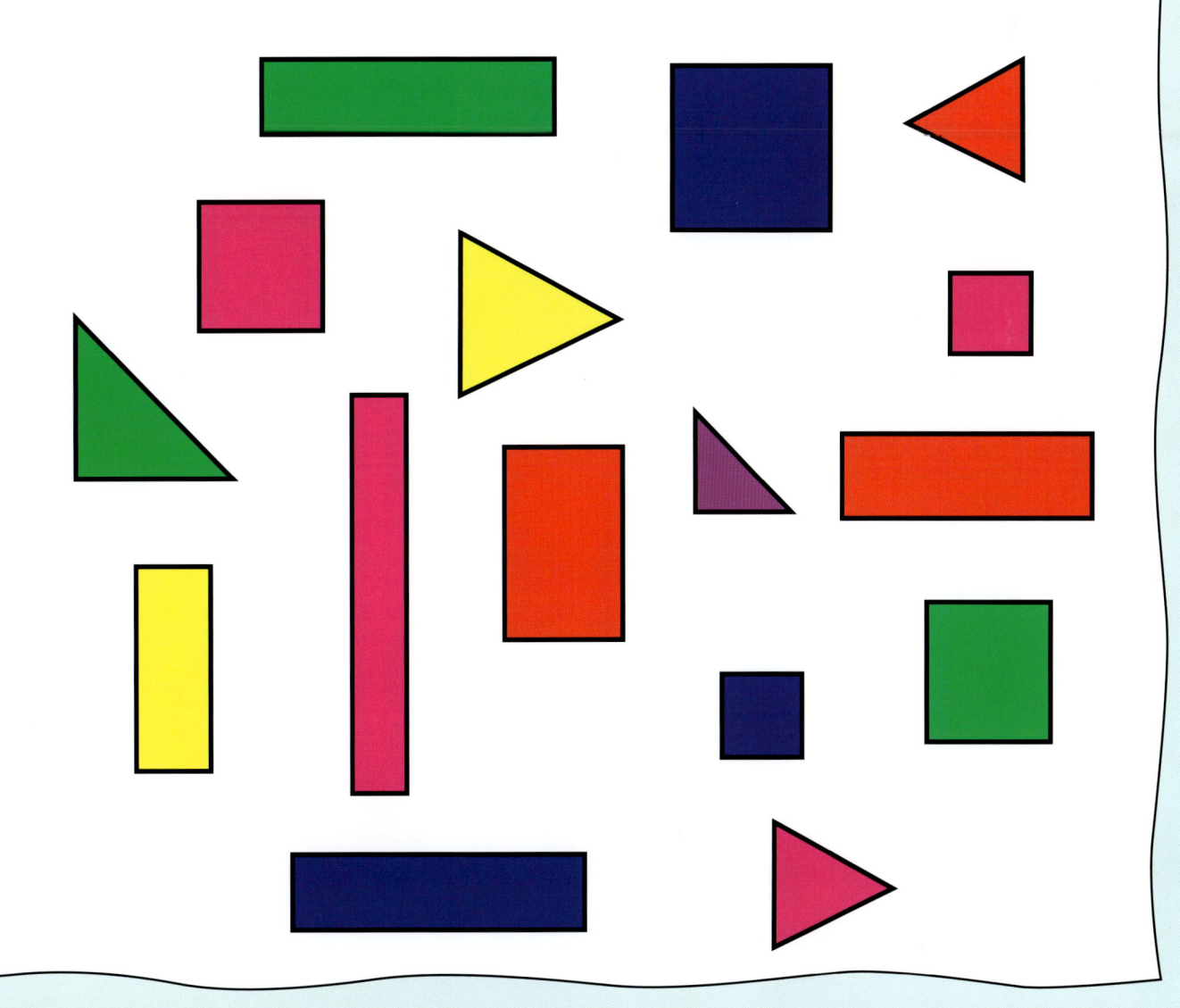

Comparing 2-D Shapes

Mind Building Math

The clowns built the silly structure below.

1. How many squares did they use? _____

2. How many circles did they use? _____

3. How many triangles did they use? _____

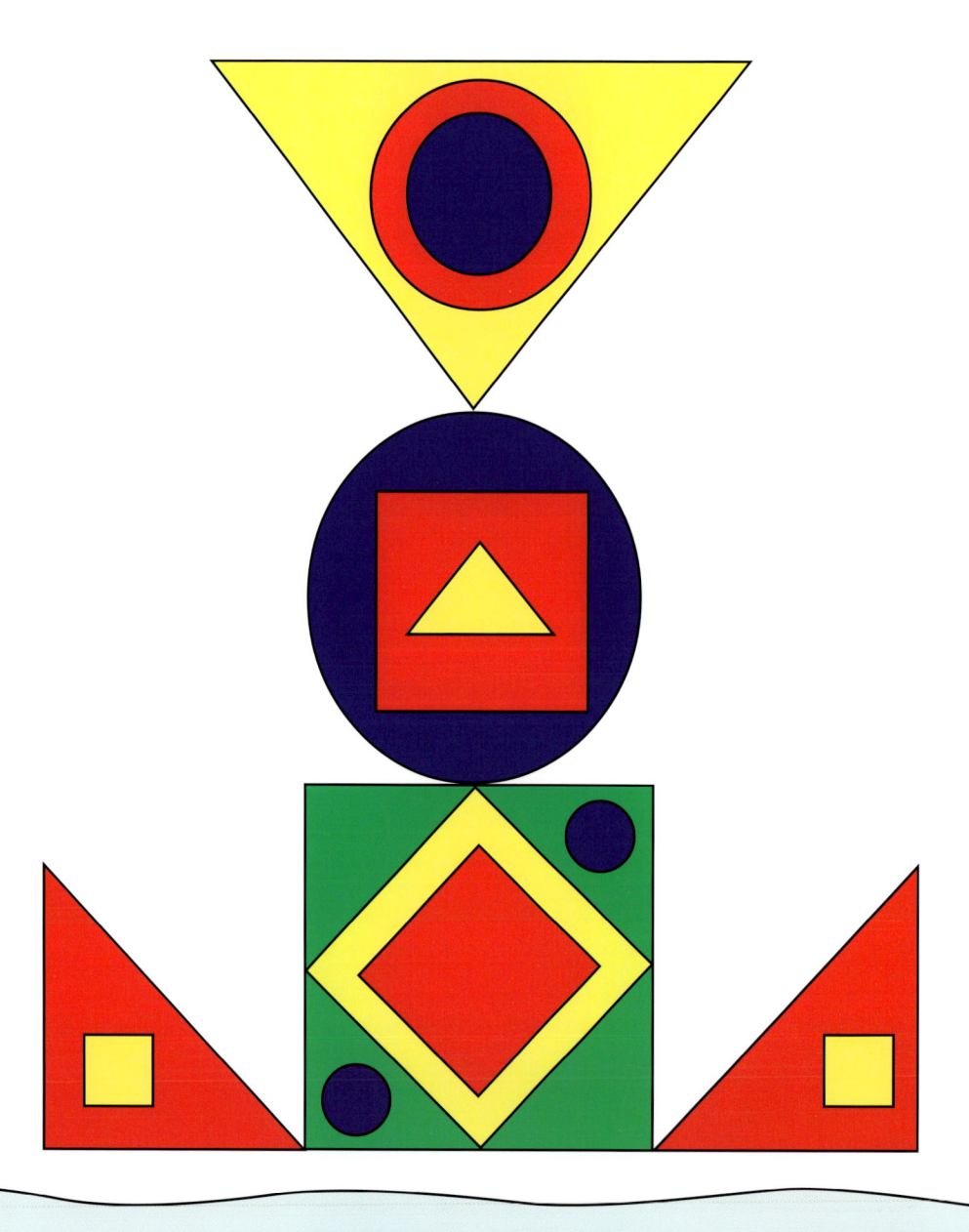

Mind Building Math

Comparing 2-D Shapes

The clowns built the silly structure below.

1. How many squares did they use? _____

2. How many circles did they use? _____

3. How many triangles did they use? _____

Comparing 2-D and 3-D Shapes

Mind Building Math

Draw a line from each object to its shadow.

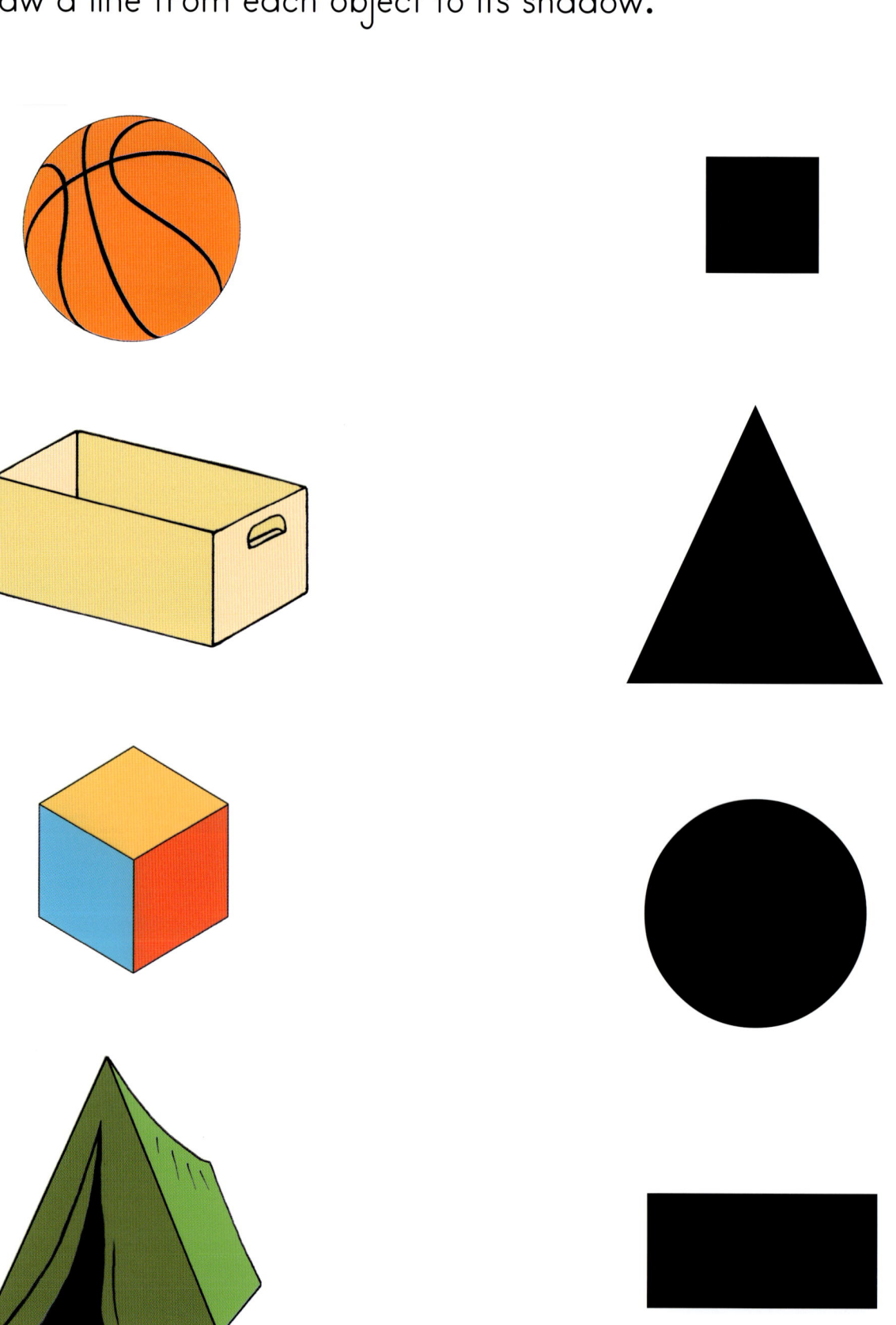

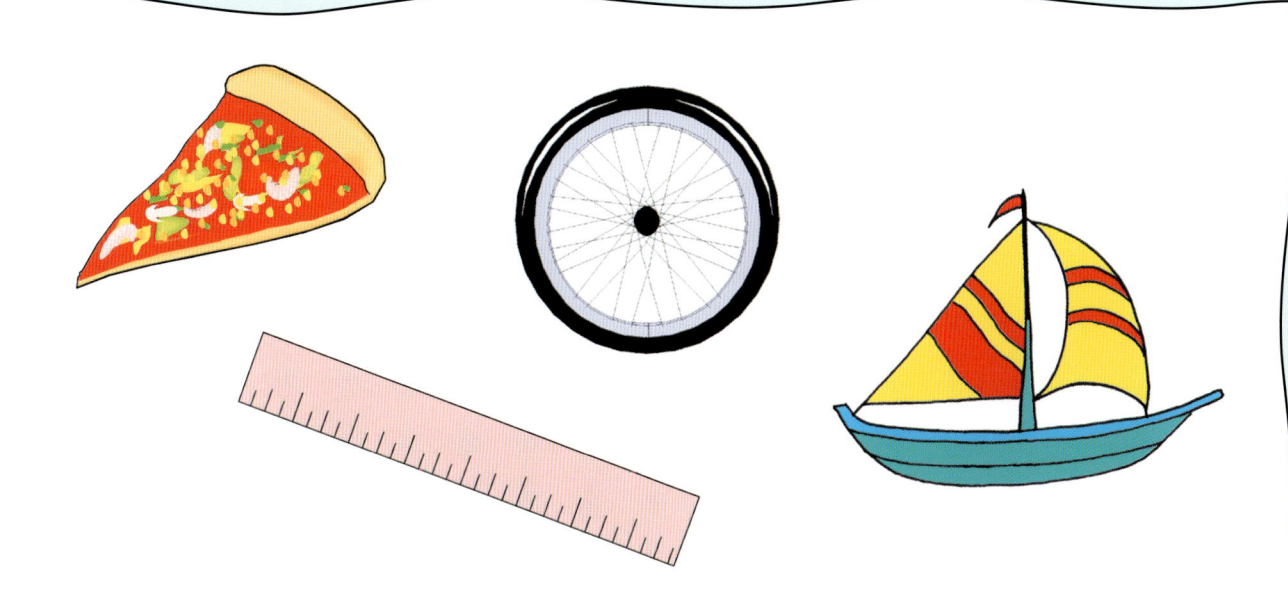

Mind Building Math

Comparing 2-D and 3-D Shapes

1. Trace around the shape that is most like the wheel.

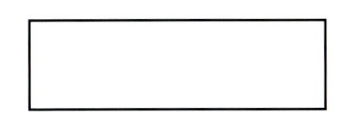

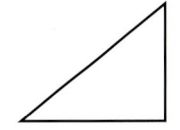

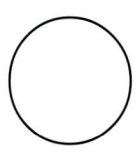

2. Trace around the shape that is most like the piece of pizza.

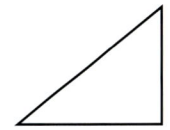

3. Trace around the shape that is most like the ruler.

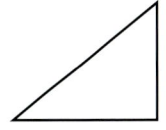

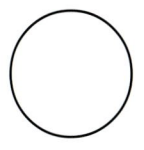

4. Trace around the shape that is most like the sail on the boat.

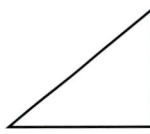

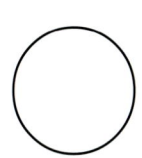

Comparing 2-D and 3-D Shapes

Mind Building Math

1. Trace around the shape that is most like the pie.

2. Trace around the shape that is most like the sandwich.

3. Trace around the shape that is most like the dollar bill.

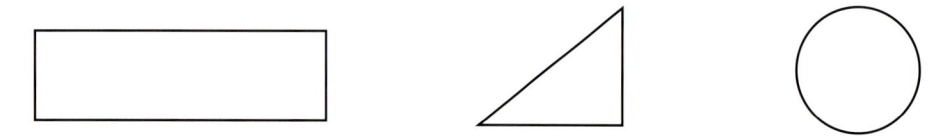

4. Trace around the shape that is most like the dolphin's top fin.

104 © 2004 The Critical Thinking Company • www.CriticalThinking.com • 800-458-4849

Mind Building Math

Shape Attributes

Circle the correct shape.

1. If [triangle] had 1 more side what could it look like?

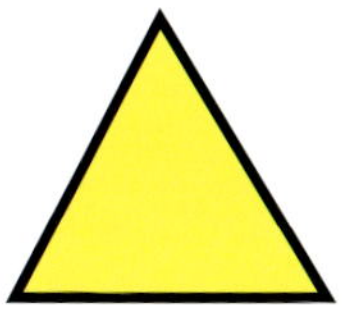

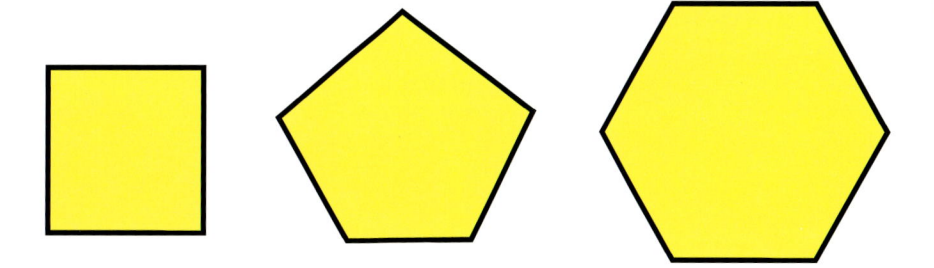

2. If [square] had 1 more side what could it look like?

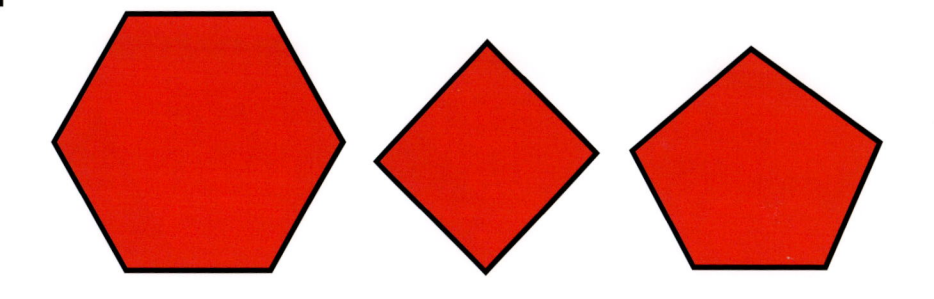

3. If [pentagon] had 1 more side what could it look like?

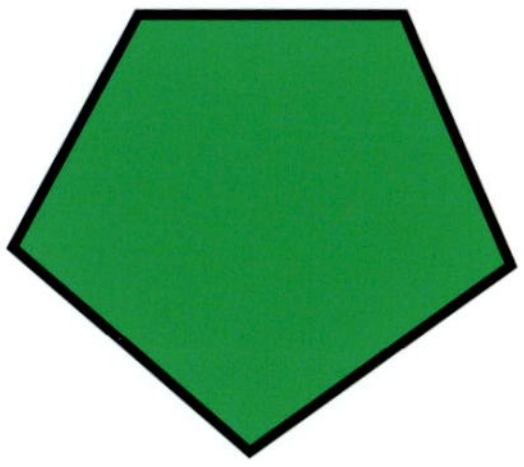

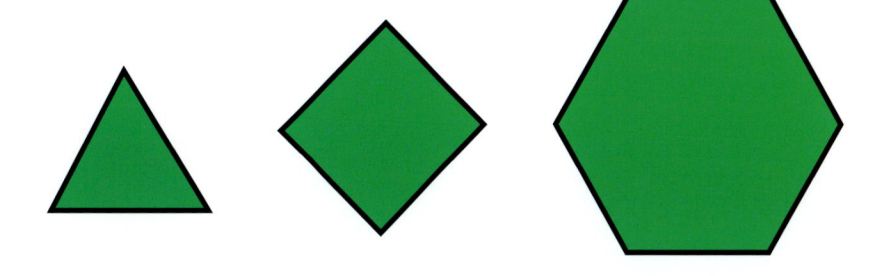

Shape Attributes

Mind Building Math

Circle the correct shape.

1. If ⬢ had 1 side fewer what could it look like?

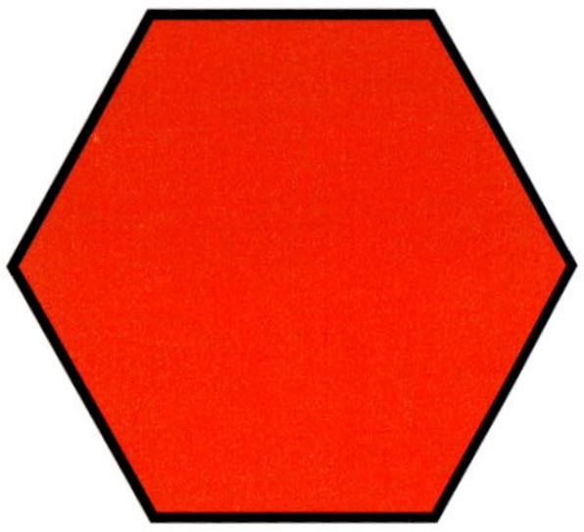

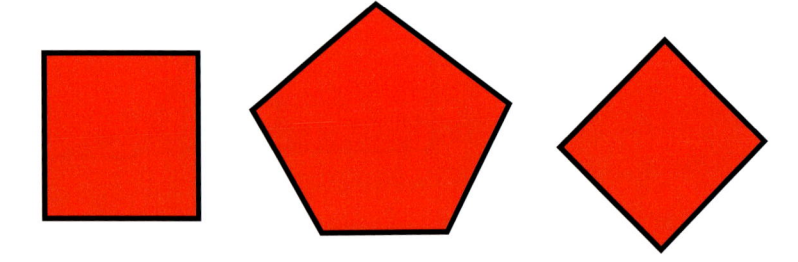

2. If 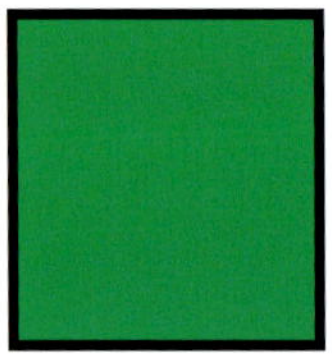 ■ had 1 side fewer what could it look like?

3. If 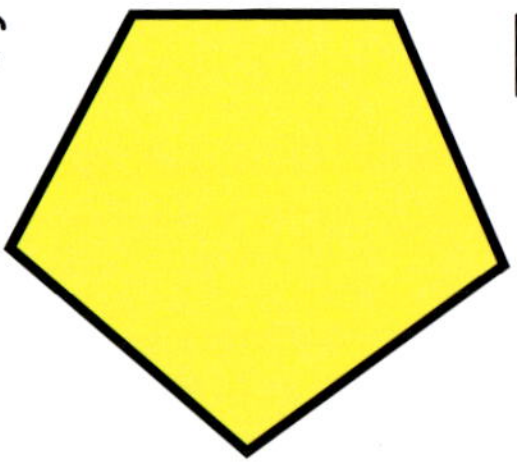 ⬟ had 1 side fewer what could it look like?

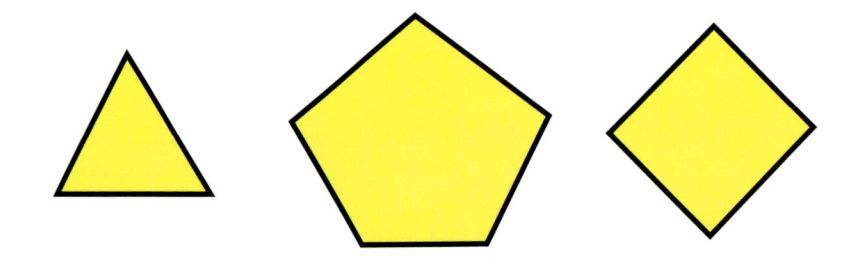

Mind Building Math

Shape Attributes

1. Draw a ● in each corner of every shape.
   Count the corners of each shape and write the number inside the shape. The first one is done for you.

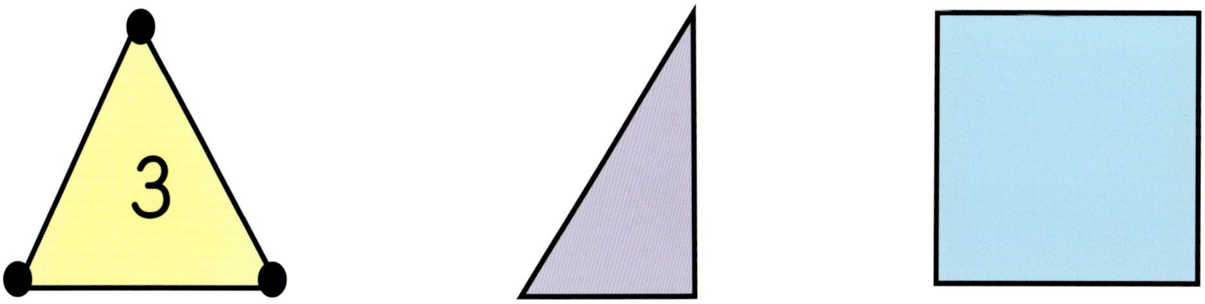

2. Now for each shape below, count its sides and write the number underneath.

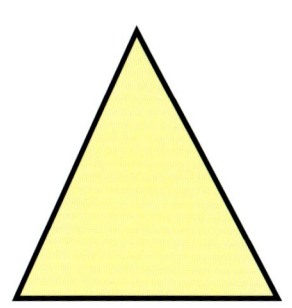

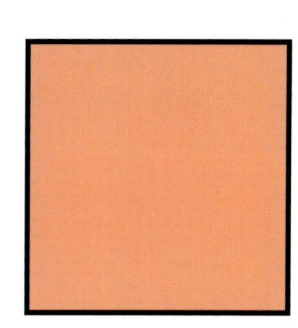

   _3_ sides   ____ sides   ____ sides

3. If a shape has 4 sides, how many corners does it have? ____

© 2004 The Critical Thinking Company • www.CriticalThinking.com • 800-458-4849

Shape Attributes   Mind Building Math

1. Draw a ● in each corner of every shape.
   Count the corners of each shape and write the number inside the shape.

2. Count the sides of each shape and write the number below each shape.

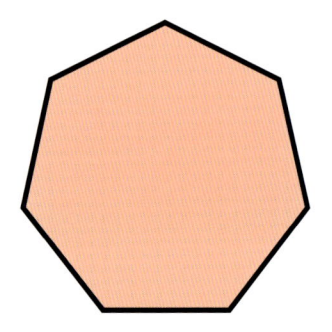

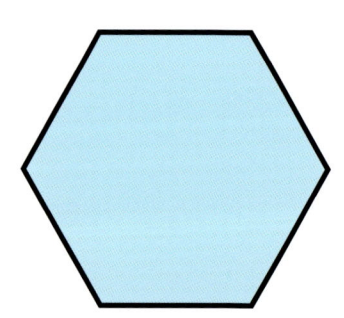

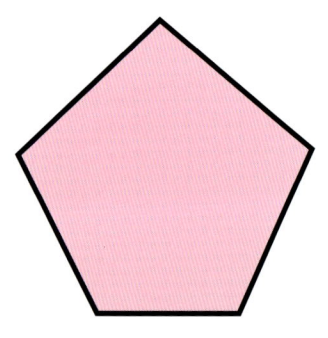

   _____ sides   _____ sides   _____ sides

3. Can a shape have 6 corners but only 5 sides?

   Yes   or   No   Explain your thinking.

4. Can a shape have 7 corners but only 6 sides?

   Yes   or   No   Explain your thinking.

108   © 2004 The Critical Thinking Company • www.CriticalThinking.com • 800-458-4849

Mind Building Math

Combining Shapes

Rabbit is building shapes.

1. Which two pieces below can he put together to make this shape? Circle them.

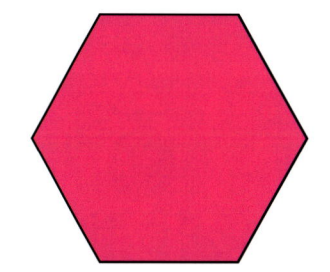

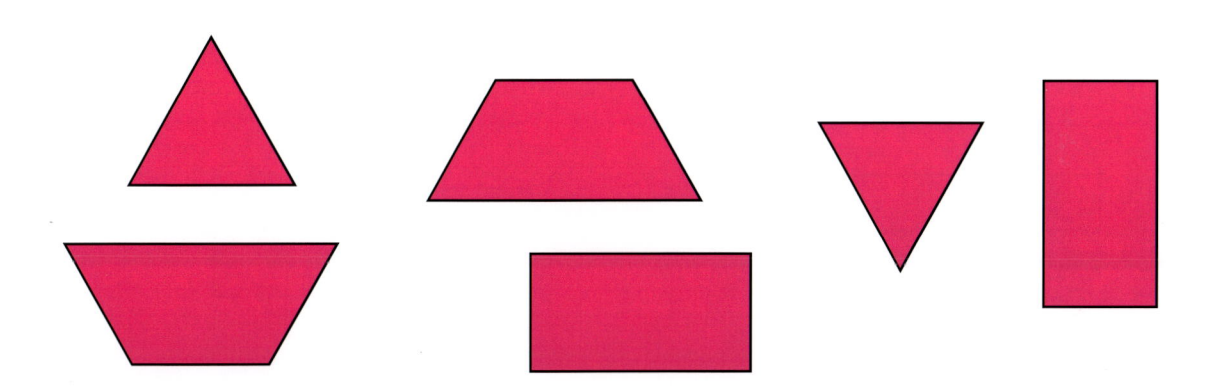

2. Which two pieces below can he put together to make this shape? Circle them.

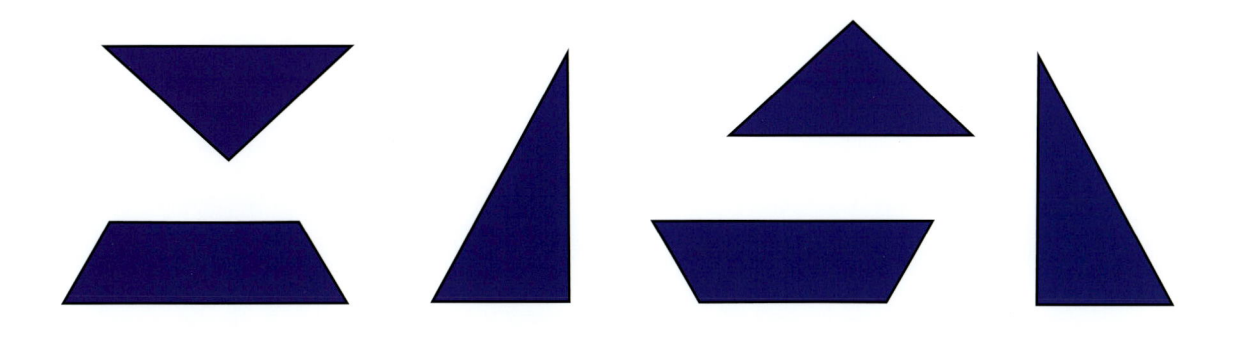

© 2004 The Critical Thinking Company • www.CriticalThinking.com • 800-458-4849

Sorting 2-D Shapes

Mind Building Math

Draw a line from each design to the set of shapes used to build it.

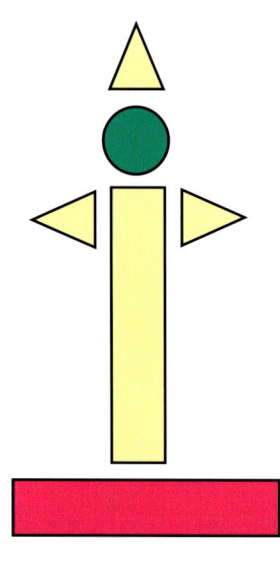

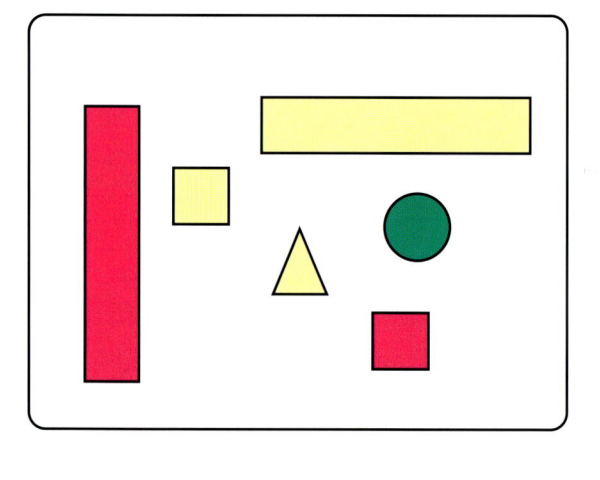

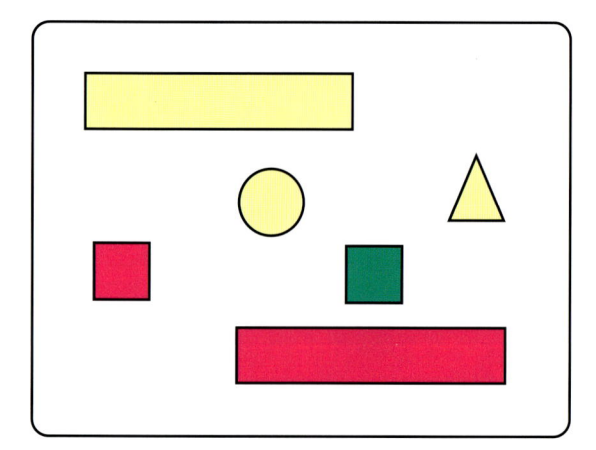

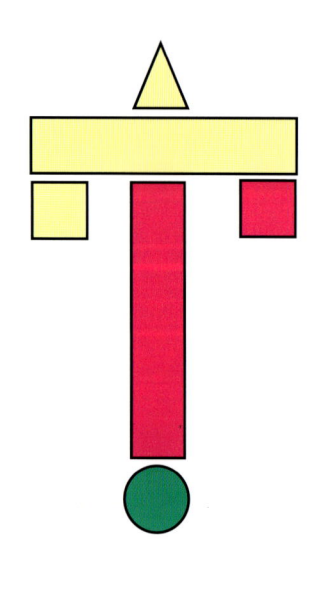

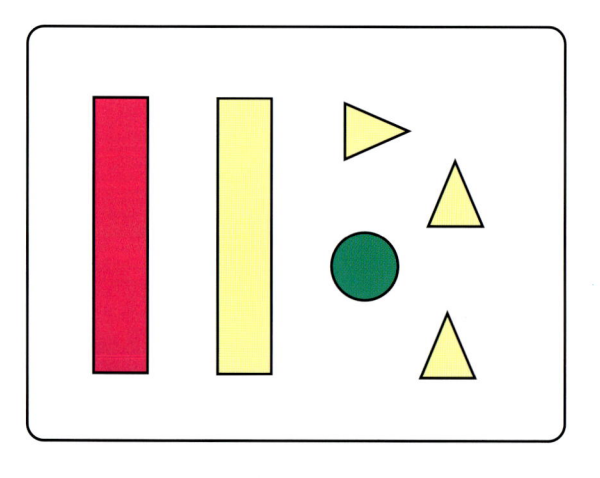

Mind Building Math

Sorting 2-D Shapes

Draw a line from each design to the set of shapes used to build it.

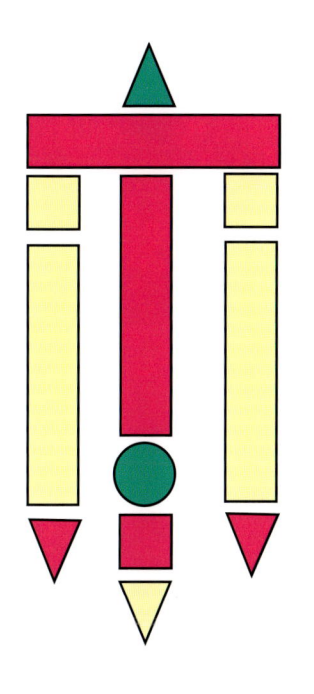

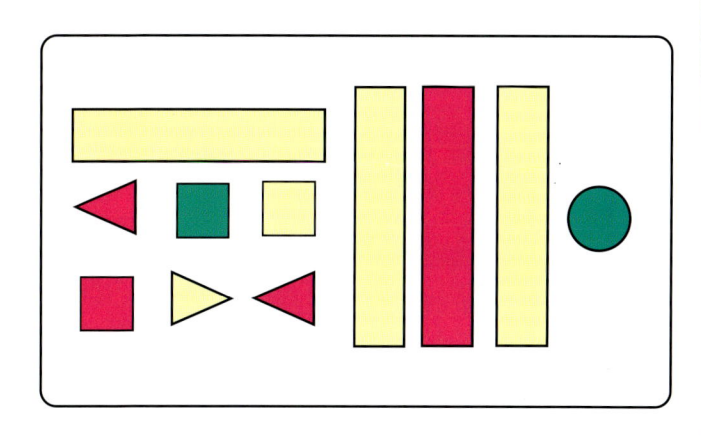

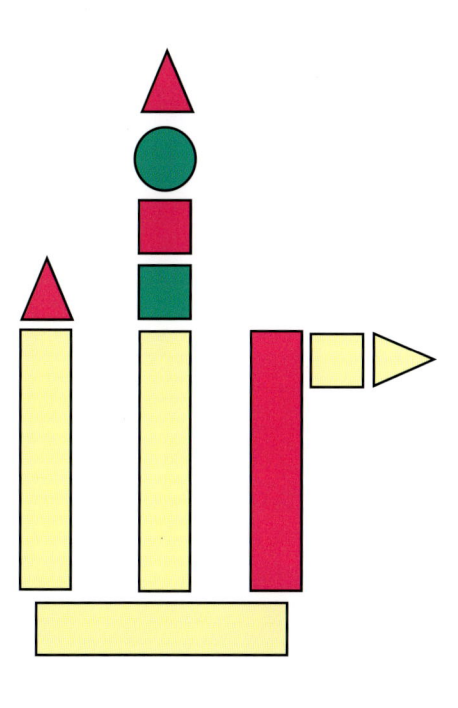

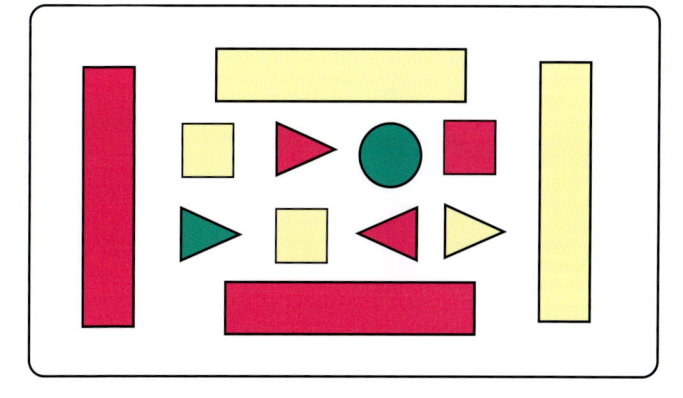

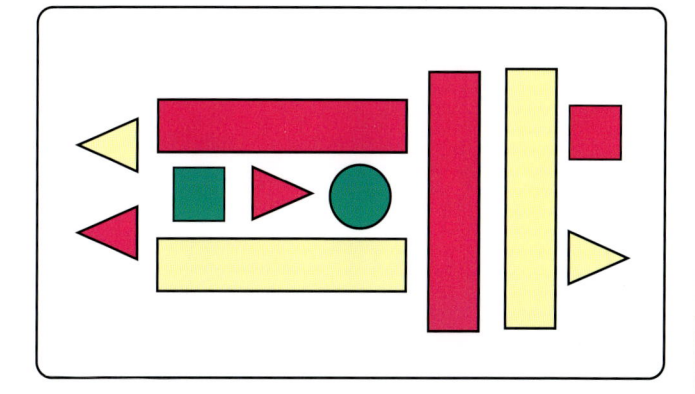

Spatial Position   Mind Building Math

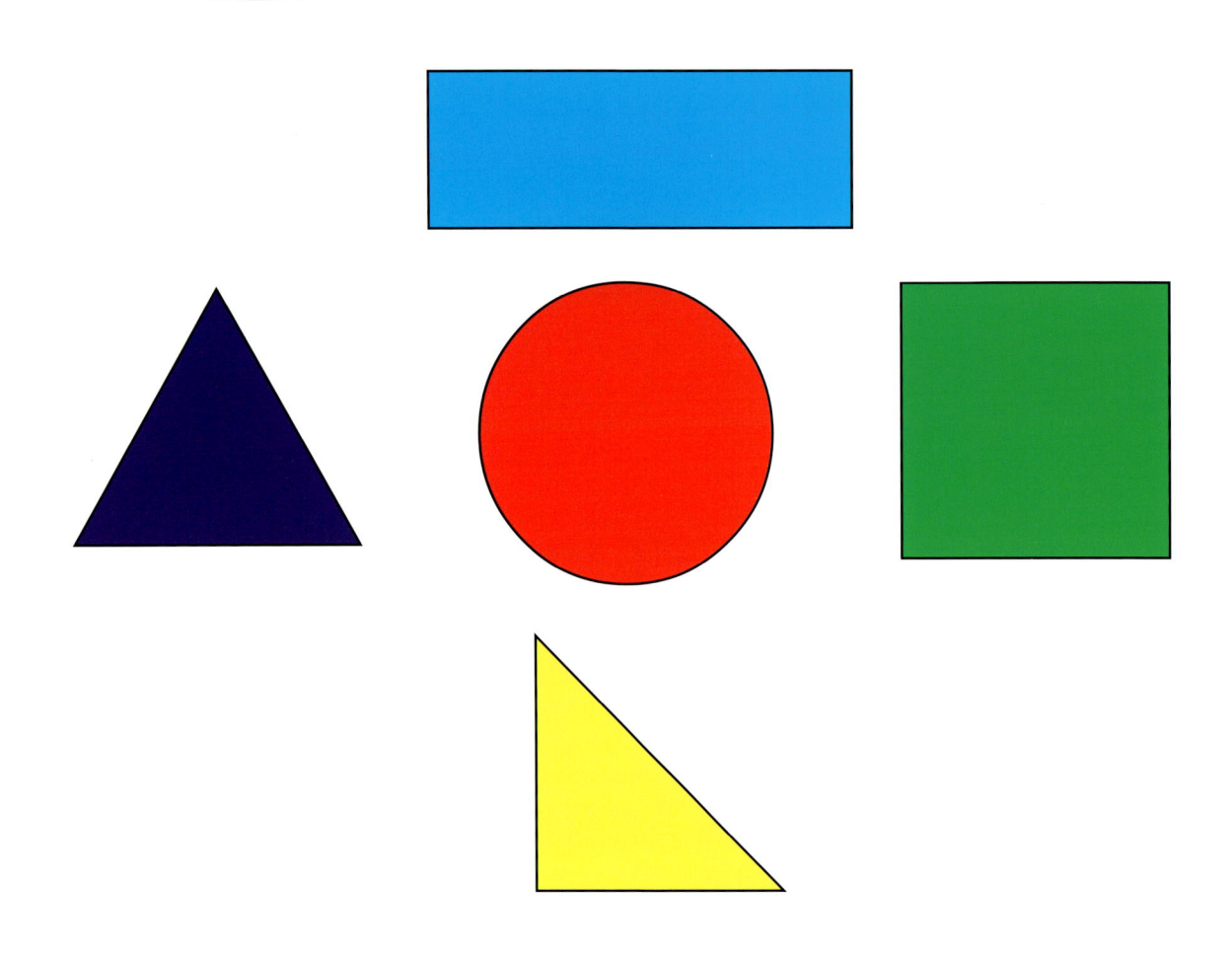

1. Which shape is above the circle?

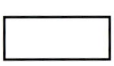

   ▢   △   ▭

2. Which shape is between the blue triangle and the square?

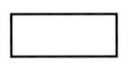

   ○   ▢   ▭

3. Draw an X on the shape that is beside a triangle.

4. Draw a circle around the shape below the circle.

Circle the correct shape to answer each question.

1. Which shape is inside the circle?

2. Which shape is outside the triangle?

3. Which shape is inside the square?

4. Which shape is outside the square?

5. Which shape is inside the rectangle?

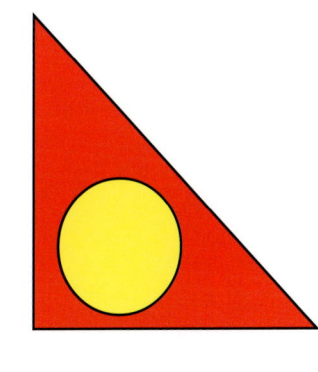

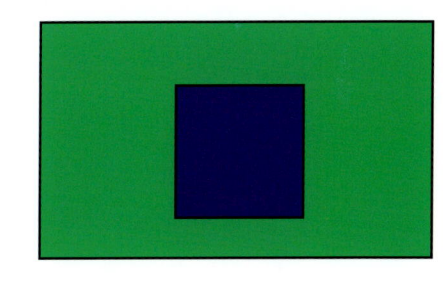

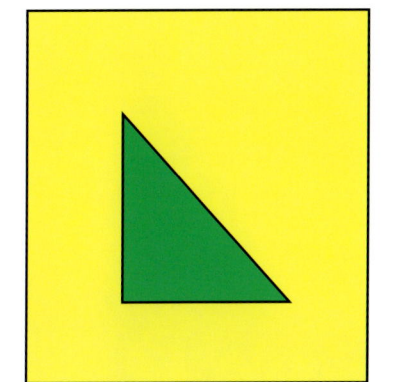

Spatial Position

Mind Building Math

1. What is under the umbrella?

2. What is beside the sand castle?

3. Draw a ball in front of the sand castle.

4. Draw a shovel between the umbrella and towel.

Left ⟷ Right

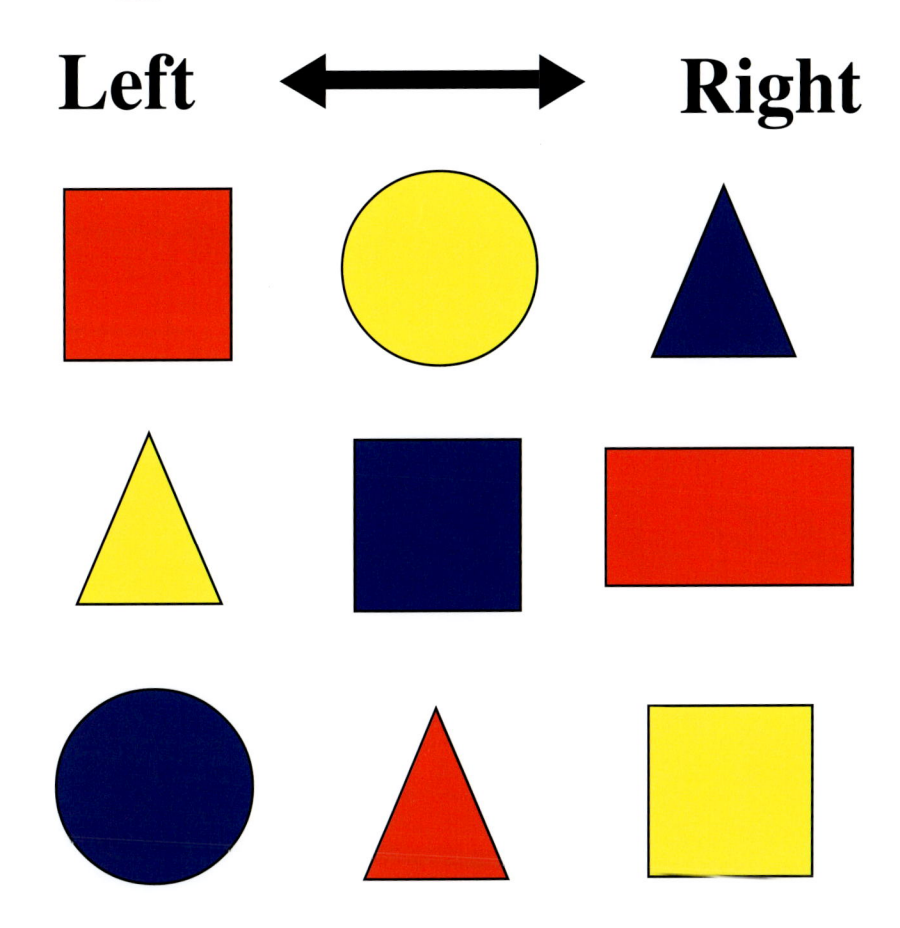

1. Draw what is to the left of the bottom square.

2. Draw what is to the left of the bottom triangle.

3. Draw what is to the right of the middle square.

4. Draw what is to the left of the top circle.

Directions Mind Building Math

1. Circle the object that is the first one to the right of the apple.

2. Put an X on the object that is the first one to the left of the ant.

3. Draw the first object to the right of the sandwich.

4. Draw the first object to the left of the lemonade.

116 © 2004 The Critical Thinking Company • www.CriticalThinking.com • 800-458-4849

Mind Building Math

Directions

Follow the directions below
to find the missing numbers.

1. Start at 2.
   Go down one space.
   Then go right one space.
   End at _____.

2. Start at 11.
   Go up one space.
   Then go left two spaces.
   End at _____.

3. Start at 4.
   Go down one space.
   Then go left two spaces.
   End at _____.

Directions Mind Building Math

Follow the directions below to help Spot find the best bones. Circle the bones you find.

1. Start at B.
   Go right one space.
   Then go down one space.
   Circle the bone you found.

2. Start at A.
   Go left two spaces.
   Then go down two spaces.
   Circle the bone you found.

3. Start at C.
   Go left one space.
   Then go up two spaces.
   Circle the bone you found.

Mind Building Math

Directions

Help Little Dragon catch food in the cave. Follow the directions as you go through the cave.

1. Start at 1.
   Go left one space.
   Then go up one space.
   Circle the bug you caught.

2. Start at 2.
   Go down two spaces.
   Then go right one space.
   Underline the bug you caught.

3. Start at 1.
   Go left two spaces.
   Then go up one space.
   Put an X on the bug you caught.

© 2004 The Critical Thinking Company • www.CriticalThinking.com • 800-458-4849

119

Comparing Height

Mind Building Math

1. Circle the elephant that is not the tallest and not the shortest one.

2. Circle the lion that is shorter than the tallest one but is taller than the shortest one.

3. Circle the giraffe that is taller than the shortest one but shorter than the tallest one.

Mind Building Math

Comparing Length

This picture shows what happened in the paper plane contest.

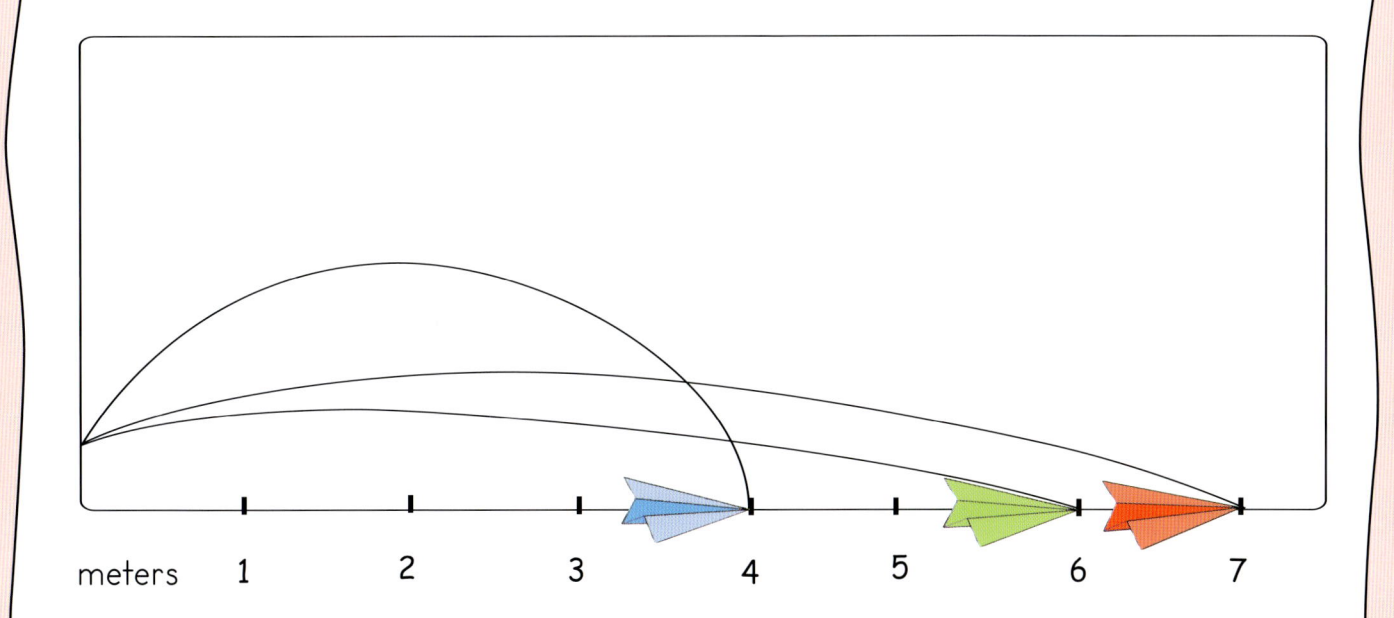

meters   1   2   3   4   5   6   7

1. Circle the plane that went farthest.

2. How far did the blue plane fly? _____ meters

3. How much farther did the green plane fly than the blue plane? _____ meters

4. Circle the plane that went highest.

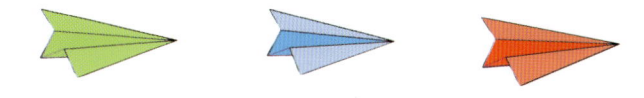

Comparing Volume   Mind Building Math

In each row, circle the object that holds more.

1.

2.

3.

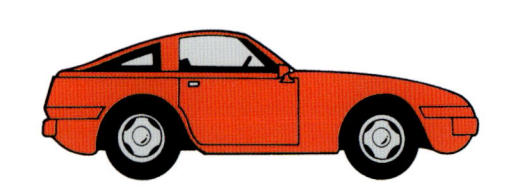

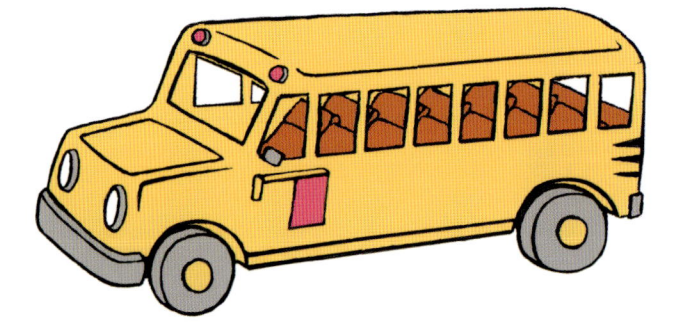

Mind Building Math

Comparing Volume

1. Could the empty jar hold more olives or fewer olives than the full jar? _____
How do you know?

2. This box holds 4 crayons.

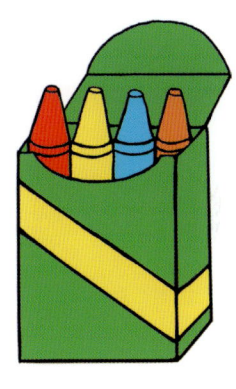

Circle the box that will hold exactly the same amount.
Put an X on the box that will hold fewer crayons.

Comparing Weight

Mind Building Math

1. Look at the picture below. Circle the side of the seesaw that has more weight on it. Tell how you know.

2. Circle the correct picture below. Tell what is wrong with the other picture.

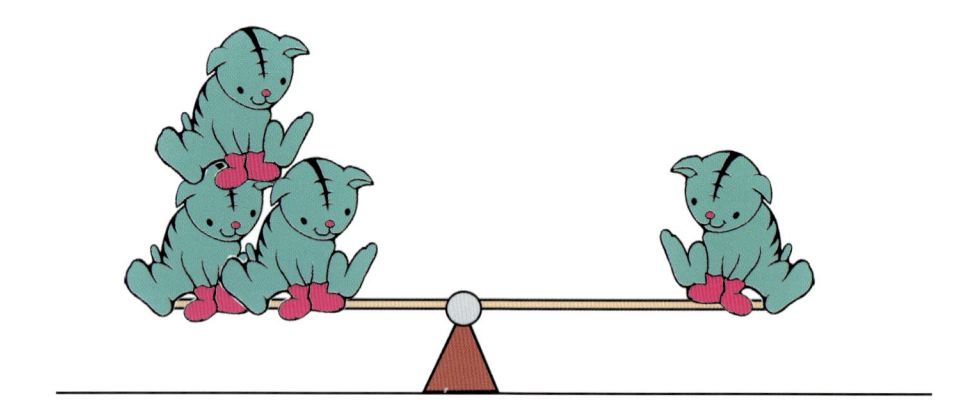

Mind Building Math — Comparing Weight

1. Look at the two seesaws below. Circle the side of each seesaw that has more weight on it. Tell how you know.

2. Circle the correct picture below. Tell what is wrong with the other picture.

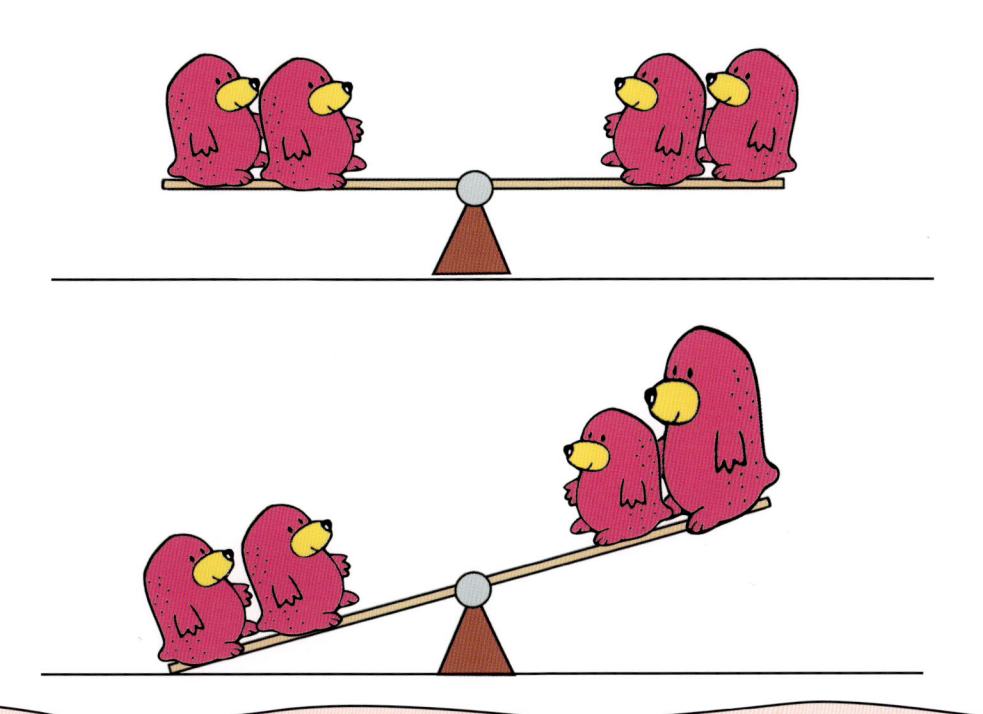

Measuring   Mind Building Math

Use the footprints to measure how long each object is.

1. The car is _____ 👣 long.

2. The bed is _____ 👣 long.

3. The bat is _____ 👣 long.

Mind Building Math

Measuring

Each 🦶 is a step. How many steps are there

1. between the frog and the squirrel? _____

2. between the dog and the bird? _____

3. between the squirrel and the bird? _____

4. Circle the animal that is the most steps away from the bird.

© 2004 The Critical Thinking Company • www.CriticalThinking.com • 800-458-4849

Measuring Tools   Mind Building Math

Draw a line from each riddle to the tool it describes.

1.

I measure minutes and hours.
I tell time using battery or electric power.
Both my hands go round and round.
Sometimes I make a ticking sound.
What am I?

2.

I measure in degrees.
Use me to see if it's going to freeze.
The higher up my red line goes
The more heat you will feel on your toes.
What am I?

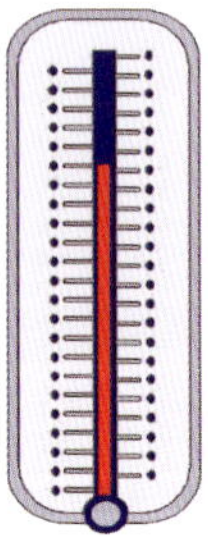

3.

I am a tool with inches and feet
but I can't even walk across the street.
Use me to measure things tall or short
and if you want to build a treetop fort.
What am I?

Mind Building Math

Telling Time

Fill in the missing numbers on the clock from 1 to 12.

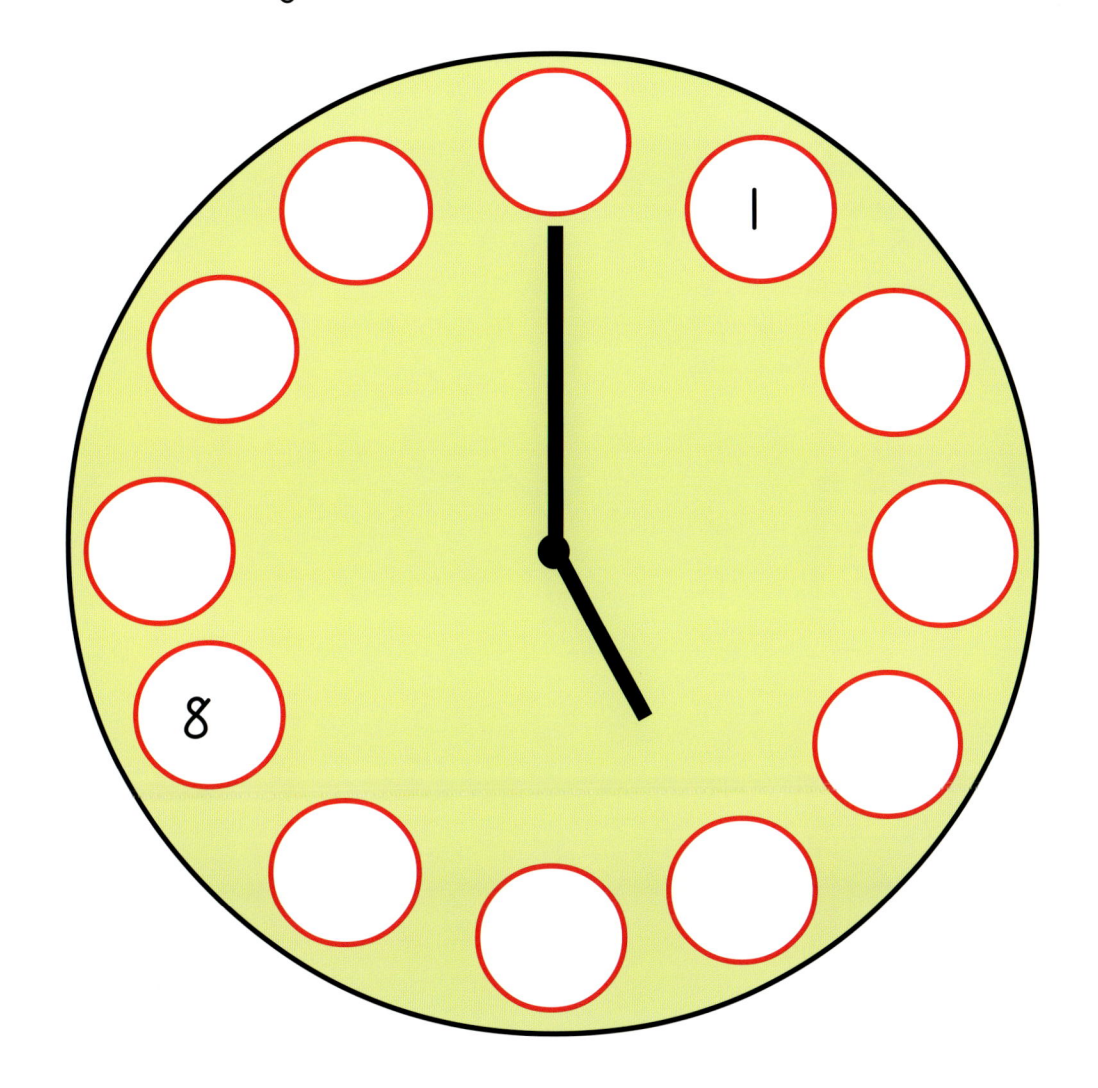

1. What number is at the top of the clock? _____

2. What number is at the bottom of the clock? _____

3. What number on the clock is after the 12? _____

4. What number is the long hand pointing to? _____

5. What number is the short hand pointing to? _____

Telling Time   Mind Building Math

Draw lines to finish matching the times to the clocks.

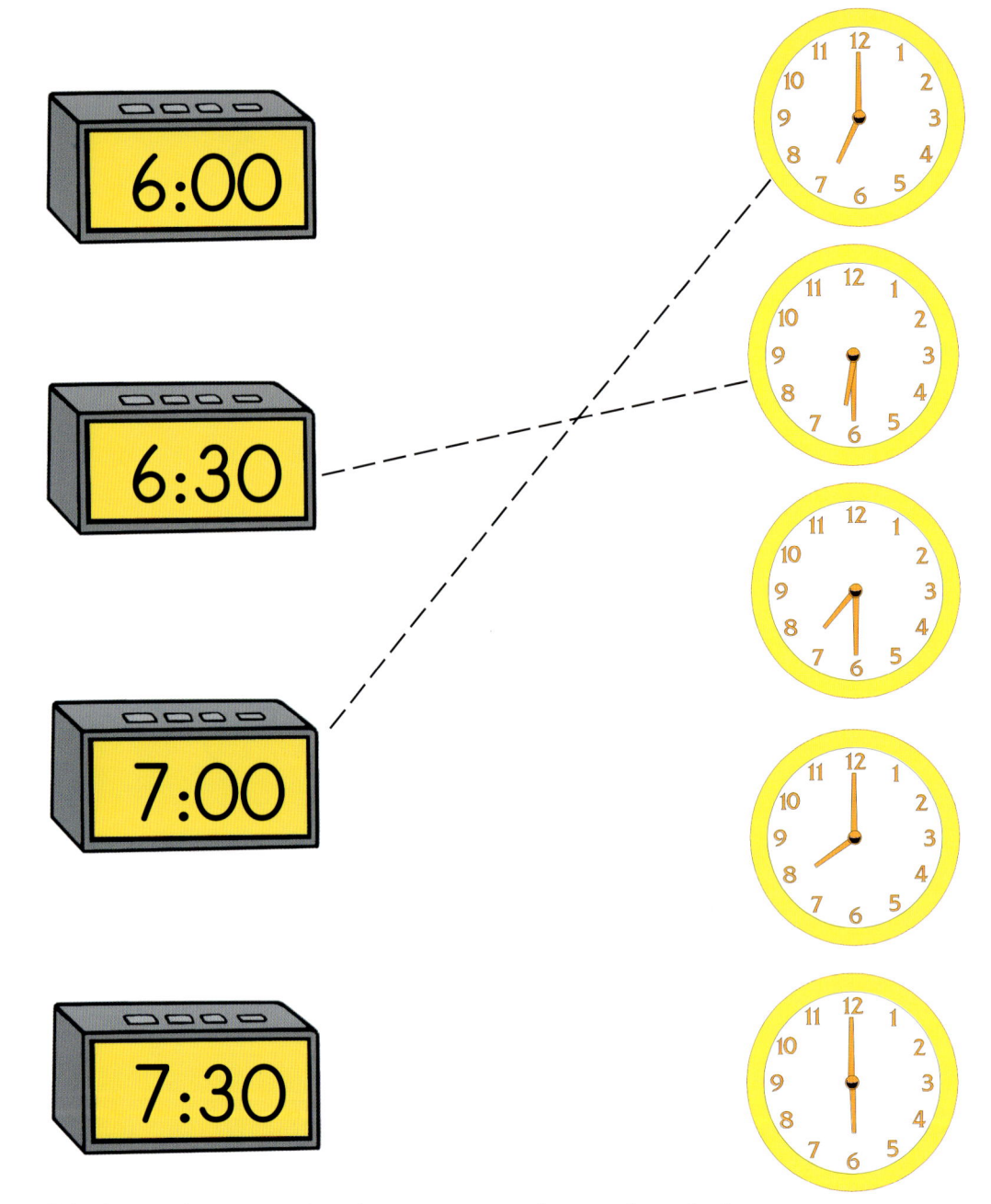

1. If the alarm clock time ends with :00, the long hand of the round clock is on _____.

2. If the alarm clock time ends with :30, the long hand of the round clock is on _____.

Mind Building Math — Telling Time

Fill in the missing times.

6:00   6:30   ____   ____

1. If the long hand is on the 12, then the time ends with _____.

2. If the long hand is on the 6, then the time ends with _____.

3. If the short hand is on the 7 and the long hand is on the 12, what time is it? _____

4. If the long hand is on the 6 and the short hand is just past the 6, what time is it? _____

Days of Week   Mind Building Math

The calendar below shows the weather for each day last week.

Sunday	Monday	Tuesday		Thursday	Friday	Saturday
☀	☀	⛅	☁	🌧	❄	⛅

1. Which day did it rain?

   Wednesday   Thursday   Friday

2. Which day did it snow?

   Thursday   Friday   Saturday

3. What was the weather like the day before Monday?

4. What was the weather like the day after Friday?

132

Mind Building Math   **Days of Week**

Sun	Mon	Tues	Wed	Thurs	Fri	Sat
		1	2	3	4	5

Circle the correct answer.

1. If today is Wednesday, what day was yesterday?

    Tues   Thurs   Mon

2. If today is Thursday, what day will it be in two days?

    Mon   Fri   Sat

3. If yesterday was Sunday, what day is it today?

    Sat   Fri   Mon

4. If tomorrow is Wednesday, what day is it today?

    Tues   Fri   Mon

5. If today is Saturday, what day is tomorrow?

    Fri   Sun   Thurs

Days of Week   Mind Building Math

The calendar shows what Manny does each day of the week.

Sunday	Monday	Tuesday	Wednesday	Thursday	Friday	Saturday
ride bike	play baseball	swim	play baseball	swim	go to library	play soccer

1. What does Manny do on Tuesday?

2. How many days does he play baseball? _____

3. How many days after riding his bike does Manny play soccer? _____

4. What does he do the day after he plays soccer?

5. Which day is the day before Manny goes to the library?

   Wednesday   Thursday   Saturday

Mind Building Math

Using Data

Each student brought his or her favorite stuffed animal to school. Use the graph to answer the questions.

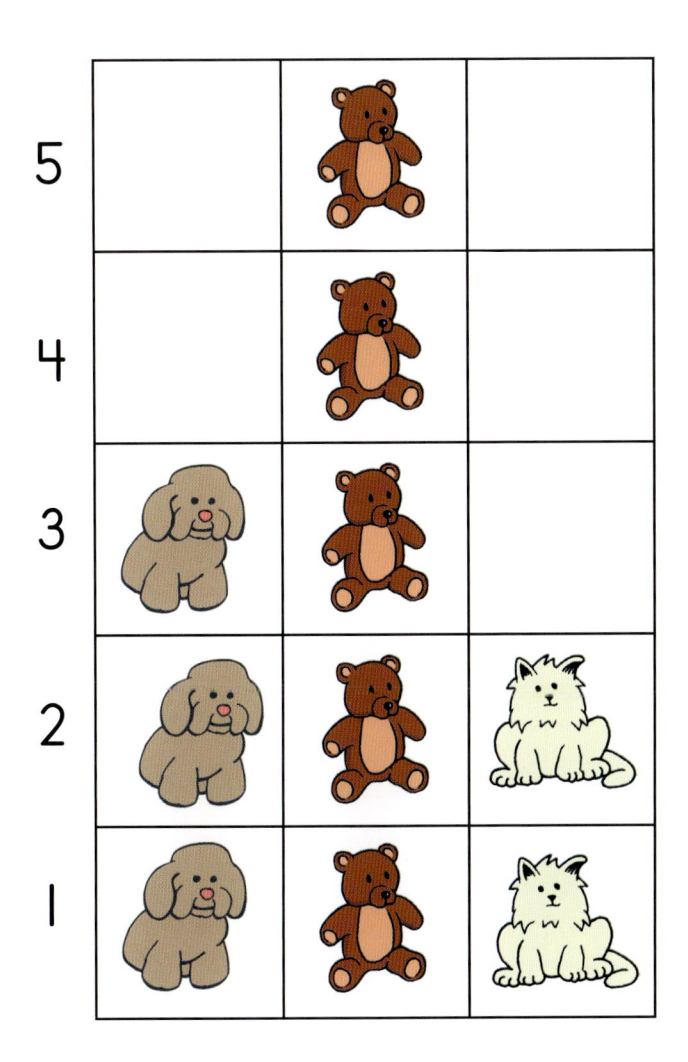

1. How many dogs are there? _____

2. Circle the kind of animal that is the fewest.

3. How many more bears are there than dogs? _____

© 2004 The Critical Thinking Company • www.CriticalThinking.com • 800-458-4849

135

Graphing   Mind Building Math

🫛	🍅	🥕	🥬	🧅
3	5	7	6	4

This chart above shows how many vegetables Rabbit ate from the garden.

Fill in boxes on the graph below to show how many of each vegetable he ate. The first one is done for you.

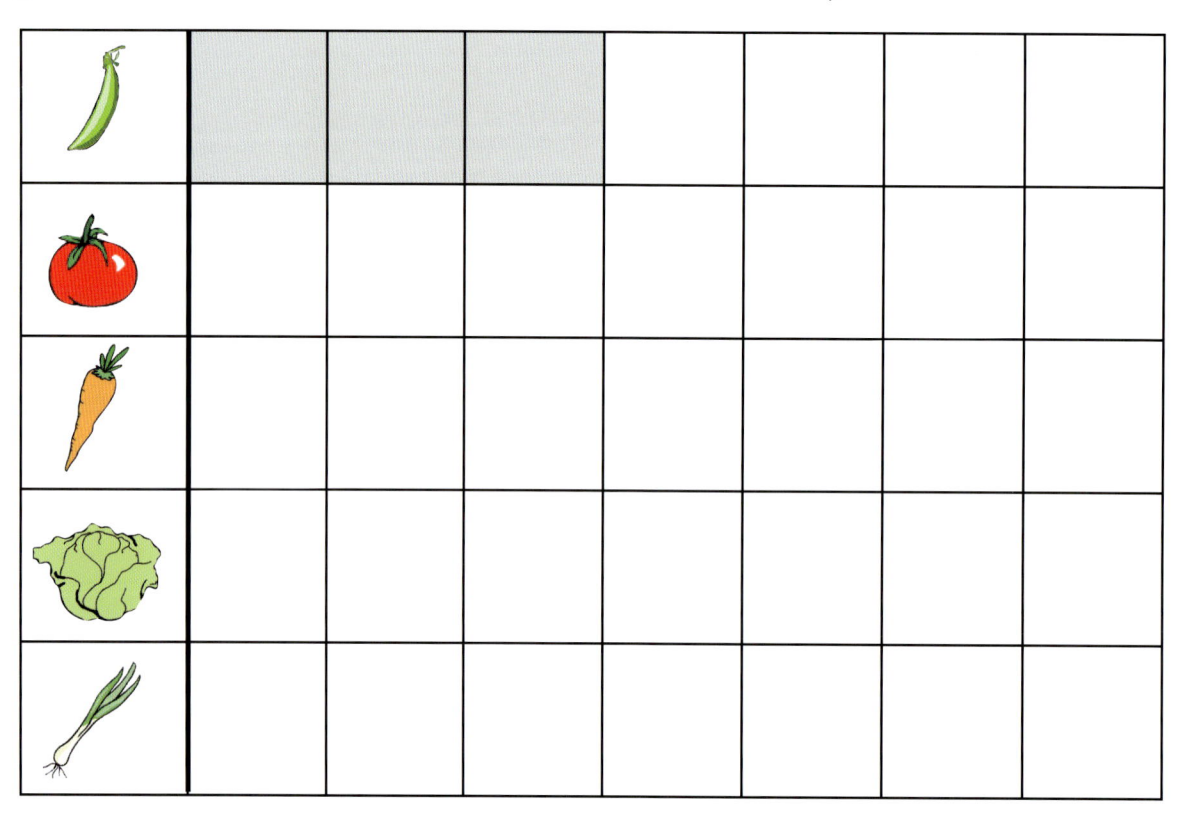

1. How many more  🥕 are there than 🍅? _____

2. How many fewer 🫛 are there than 🧅? _____

Mind Building Math — Graphing

Fill in the boxes on the graph to show the following:

   3 children liked strawberry
   5 children liked chocolate
   6 children liked vanilla

OUR FAVORITE KINDS OF ICE CREAM

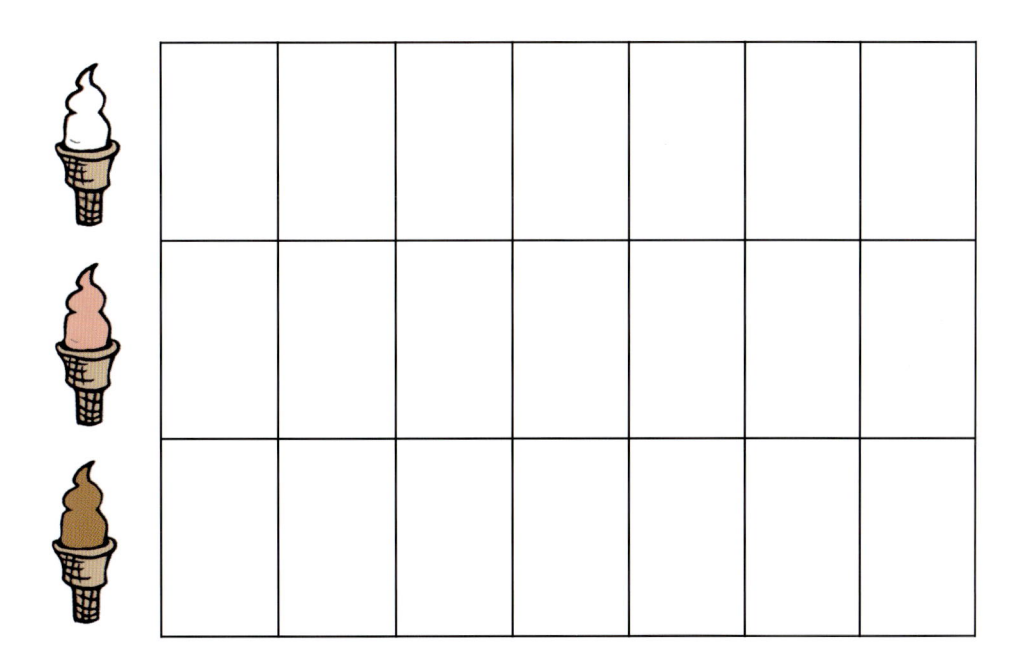

1. Put an X on the flavor that was the most favorite.

2. Circle the kind that was the least favorite.

Sorting/Graphing

Mind Building Math

Seven friends bought these treats at the movies.

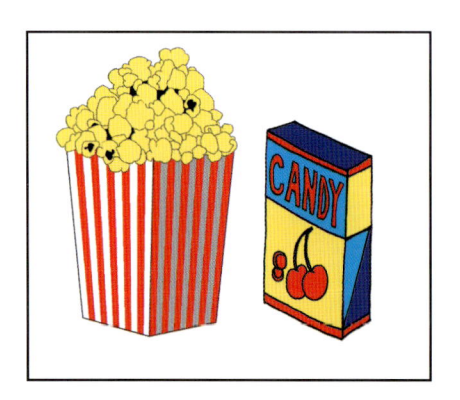

Mind Building Math

Sorting/Graphing

Shade the squares on the graph to show the number of each kind of treat that was bought.

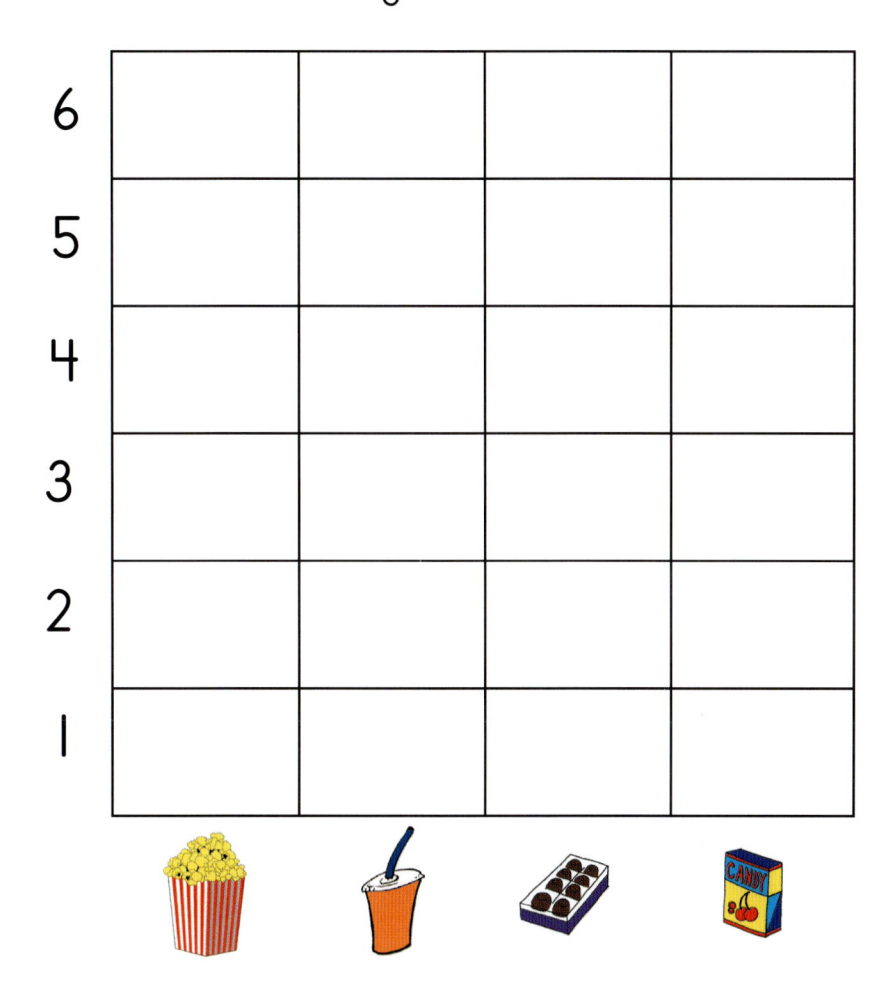

6
5
4
3
2
1

1. How many boxes of popcorn were bought? _____

2. Circle the treat that was bought the most.

3. Put an X on the treat that was bought the least.

4. How many more boxes of chocolates were bought than boxes of cherry candy? _____

Jen asked her friends to raise one hand if they liked summer ☀ best or raise both hands if they liked winter ❄ best.

Mind Building Math

Sorting/Graphing

Color or shade the graph to show which season the students liked best.

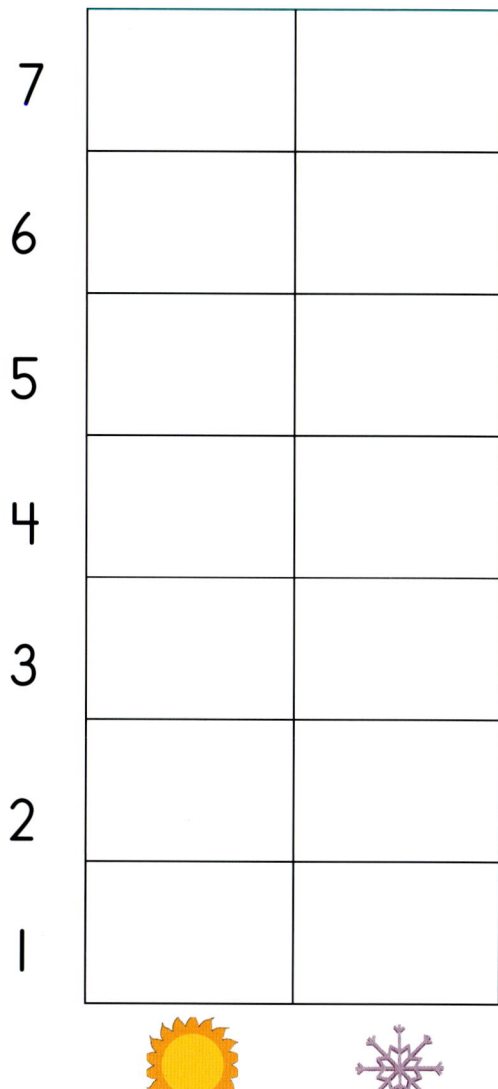

1. How many students did Jen ask? _____

2. How many students liked summer best? _____

3. How many students liked winter best? _____

4. How many students didn't like either best? _____

Graphing   Mind Building Math

Draw balls to show the following:

There are more red balls than blue balls.
There are fewer green balls than blue balls.

Green	
Blue	
Red	

Mind Building Math   Using Venn Diagram

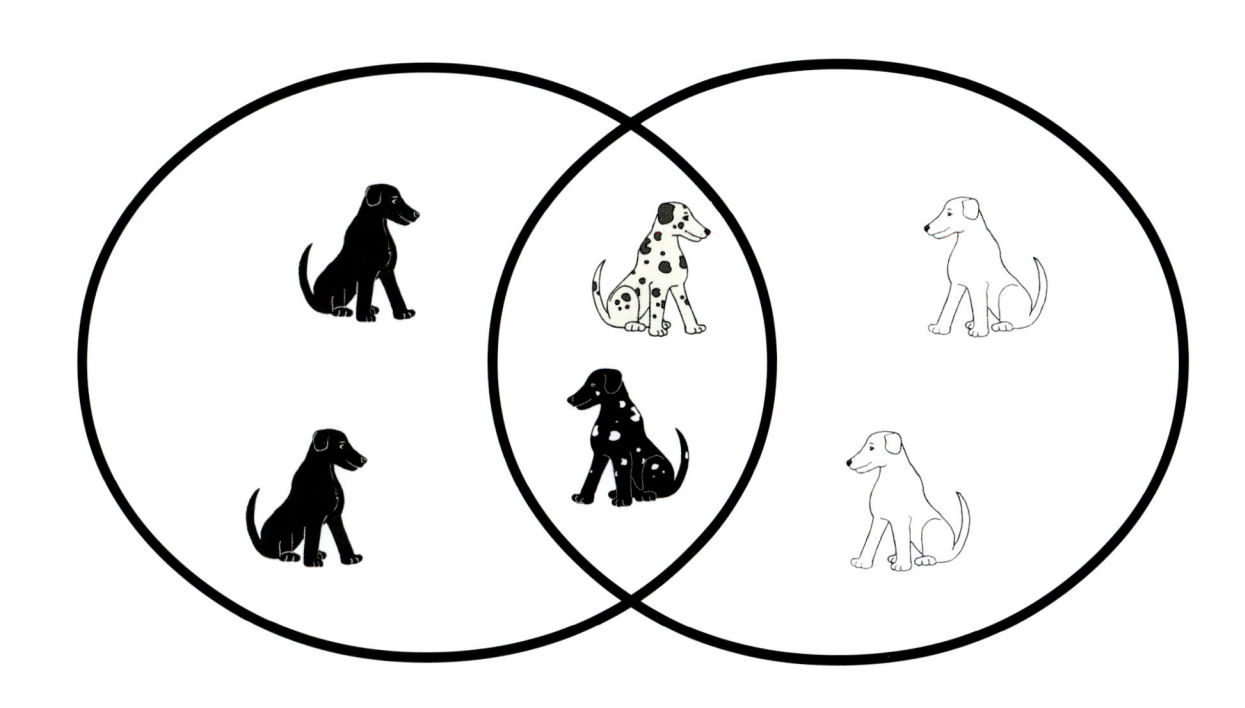

1. How many dogs are all black? _____

2. How many dogs are all white? _____

3. How many dogs are both black and white? _____

© 2004 The Critical Thinking Company • www.CriticalThinking.com • 800-458-4849

Jim can wear shirts that are all blue. Juan can wear shirts that are all yellow. Zack can wear shirts that are both blue and yellow.

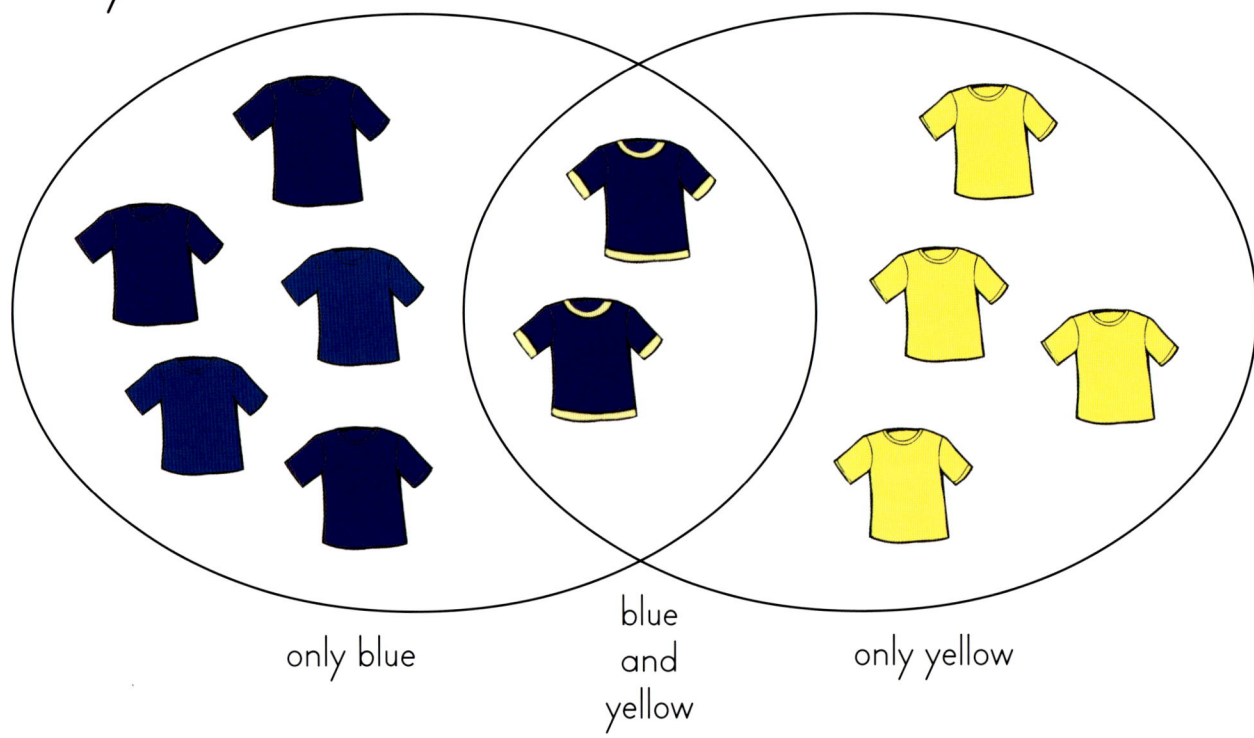

only blue   blue and yellow   only yellow

1. How many of these shirts can Jim wear? _____

2. How many of these shirts can Zack wear? _____

3. Who can wear more shirts?

   Jim   Juan   Zack

4. Who could wear this shirt?

   Jim   Juan   Zack

Sort the clowns.

One circle below is for the clowns wearing dots. The other circle is for the clowns wearing stripes. Where the circles overlap each other is for the clowns wearing both dots and stripes.

Draw lines from each clown to the circle he belongs in.

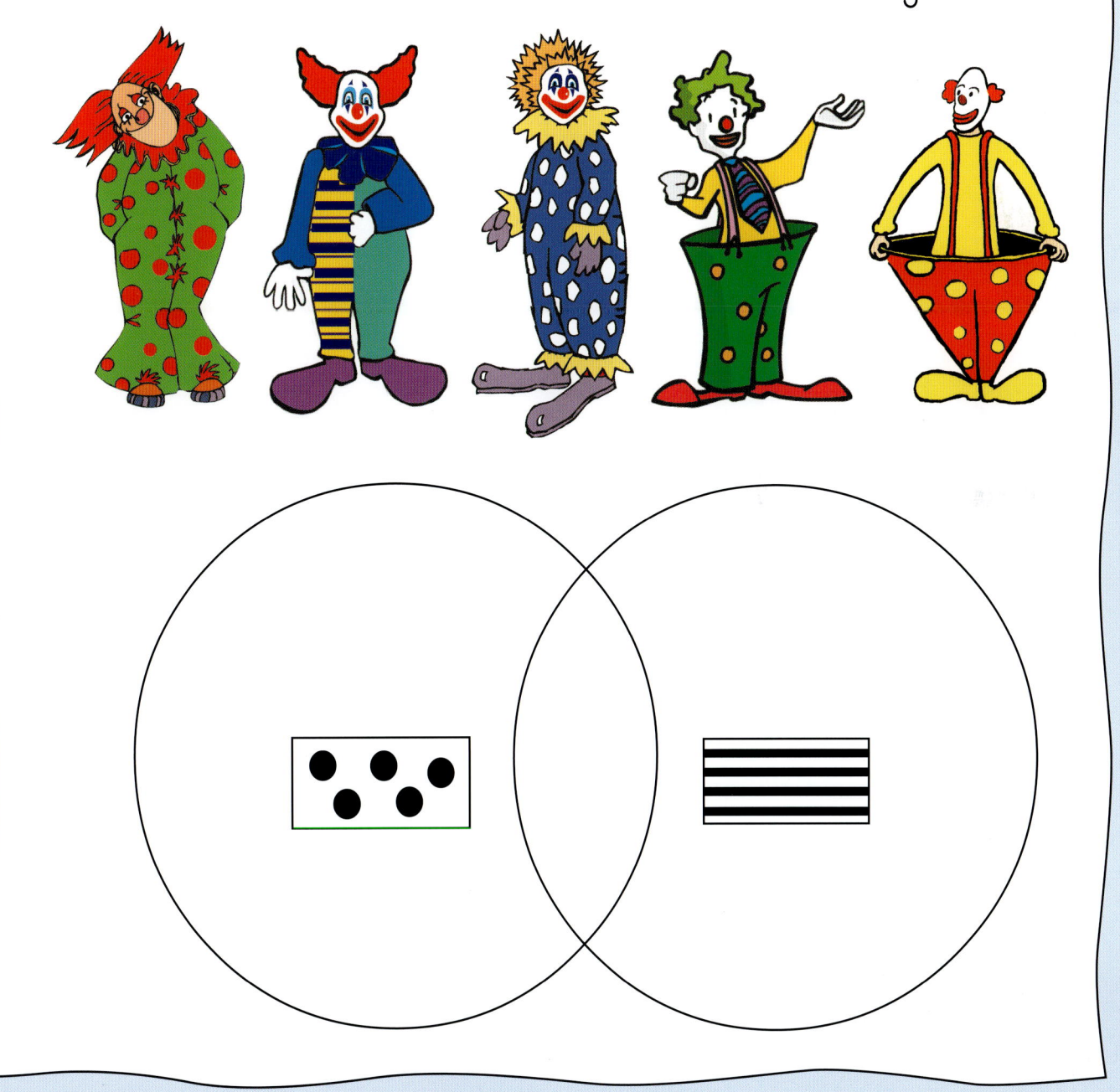

Answers

NUMBERS & OPERATIONS

Page 1

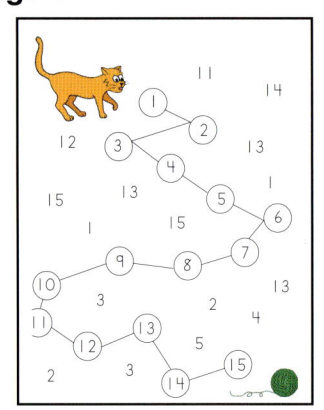

Page 2
1. carrot
2. lettuce
3. 8
4. 10

Page 3

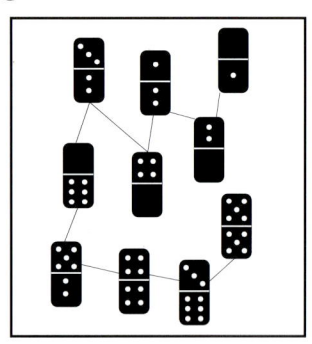

Page 4
1. ladybug
2. ladybug
3. 5
4. 12

Page 5

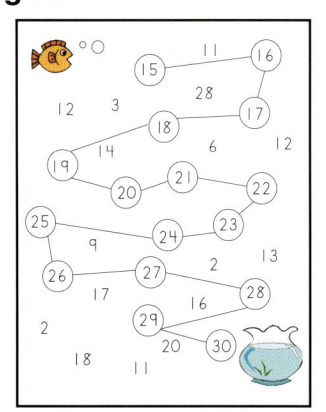

Page 6
1. 4
2. 4
3. 7
4. 5
5. 7

Page 7
1. 6
2. 6
3. 8
4. 5
5. 6

Pages 8–9
1. 5
2. Circle 10 hats.
3. 5
4. Possible answers:
   "5, because even if a dragon has two mouths, it is still just one dragon."
   "10, because every mouth can eat a cookie."

Page 10
1. Write 5 below seat 5.
2. Circle seat after brown-haired boy.
3. 4
4. 9
5. 1

Page 11
1. 8
2. 10
3. 7

Page 12
1. 6
2. 6 (Acceptable:10 if child explains that 5 buildings are the shortest compared to the 6 tallest buildings)
3. 11
4. 6

Page 13
10
Draw 2 gumballs beside each penny and number 1–10.

Page 14
1. 1, 3, 5
2. 2, 7, 9
3. 5, 8, 10

Page 15
1. 2
2. 5
3. 8
4. 6

Page 16
1. 12, 15, 17
2. 20, 22, 26
3. 23, 28, 29

Page 17
1. 3, 5, 7, 9
2. 19, 16, 14, 12

Page 18
1. 4
2. 5
3. 2
4. 8

Page 19
1. ○   2. △
3. △   4. ▭

Page 20
1. Wendy
2. Lee
3. black
4. 4th

Page 21
1. 4
2. 5
3. 8
4. 7

Mind Building Math — Answers

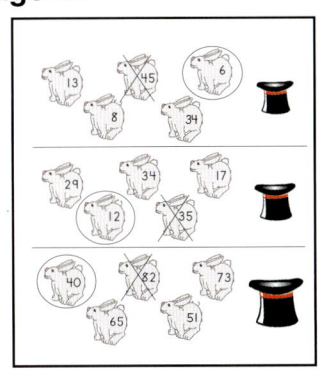

Page 22

(image of rabbits with numbers and hats)

Page 23

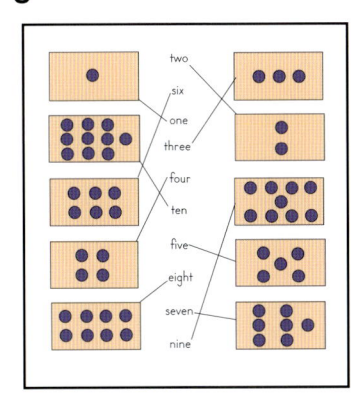

(image of dot cards matched to number words)

Page 24
1. 2
2. 4
3. 5

Page 25
1. Circle the spotted chicken.
2. 1
3. 19

Page 26

(image of penguins matched to groups of fish)

Page 27

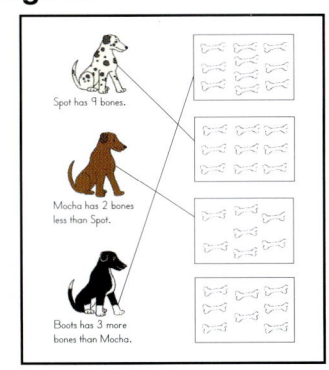

(image of dogs matched to groups of bones)

Pages 28–29
1. <u>10</u> soldiers, <u>11</u> planes, <u>9</u> trucks, <u>10</u> crowns
2. crowns
3. planes
4. trucks

Pages 30–31
1. <u>10</u> bats, <u>10</u> helmets, <u>9</u> gloves, <u>11</u> balls
2. helmets
3. balls
4. gloves

Page 32
1. Bobo 5, Coco 8, Jojo 7
2. Coco
3. 3
4. 2

Page 33

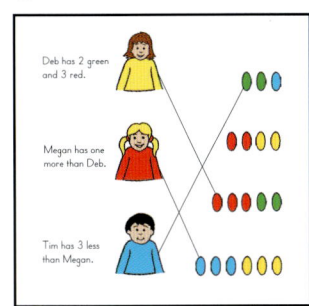

(image of children matched to groups of colored beads)

Page 34

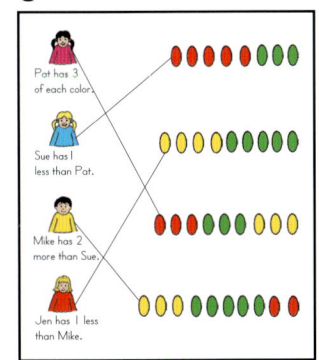

(image of children matched to groups of colored beads)

Page 35
1. 6
2. first
3. <u>2</u> blue, <u>1</u> black/white, <u>2</u> yellow, <u>1</u> orange

Page 36
1. 30
2. 50

Page 37
1. yellow fish
2. <u>2</u> red fish, <u>3</u> spotted fish, <u>6</u> yellow fish

Page 38
1. 20, 10
2. 19, 11

Page 39
1. Circle two sets of 4 clowns.
2. 2

Page 40
1. 1
2. 2
3. 4

Page 41
4. Circle four groups of 4 cars each.

Page 42
1. 3
2. 2
3. yes, 2
4. 9

Page 43
1. 2
2. yes, 1
3. 8

Page 44
1. 1
2. 4
3. 2
4. 4

© 2004 The Critical Thinking Company • www.CriticalThinking.com • 800-458-4849

Answers

Page 45
1. 20
2. 2

Page 46
1a. 6
1b. 7
2a. 5
2b. 6
2c. 7

Page 47
1. 4
2. 7
3. 7 candles on cake

Page 48

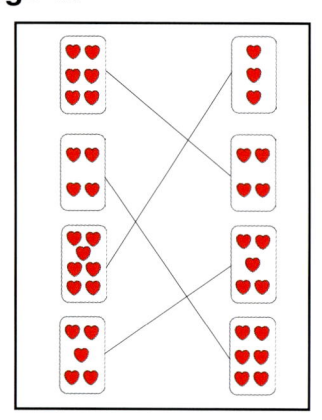

Page 49

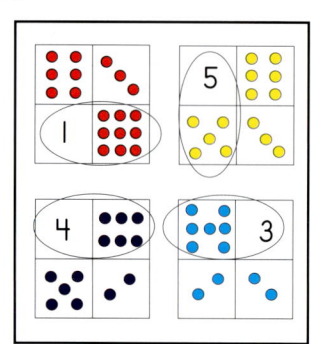

Page 50

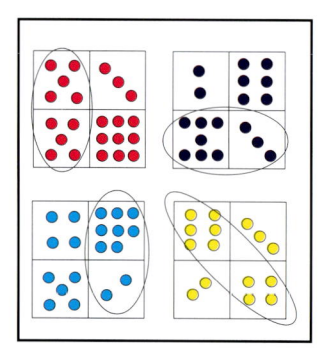

Page 51
1. 7 beads, add 3
2. 6 beads, add 4
3. 5 beads, add 5

Page 52
<u>5</u> ants
<u>7</u> ladybugs
<u>7</u> worms

Page 53
1. 9 + <u>1</u> = 10
2. 7 + <u>3</u> = 10
3. 4 + <u>6</u> = 10

Page 54
1. 3; <u>3</u> + <u>3</u> = 6
2. 3; <u>5</u> + <u>3</u> = 8

Page 55
1. 2; <u>6</u> + <u>2</u> = 8
2. 3; <u>3</u> + <u>7</u> = 10

Page 56
1. 3 balls
2. 5 balls
3. 6 balls
4. 4 balls

Page 57
1. 3
2. 8
3. 9
4. Circle fish 4 and 6

Page 58
1. 6
2. 8
3. 7
4–5. Circle or X on apple & lemon; banana & orange.

Page 59
1. 3
2. 5
3. 3

Page 60
1. 5
2. 5

Page 61
1. 6 + 7 = 13
2. <u>6</u> + 2 = <u>8</u>
3. 7 − 1 = 6

Page 62
1. 3
2. 3

Page 63
1. 7
2. 2
3. Ben

Page 64
1. 14
2. 8
3. 6

Page 65
1. 2
2. 3

Page 66
1. 13
2. 2

Page 67
10

Page 68
1. 8
2. 3 As, 2 Bs, 1 C
3. 2
4. Ann

Page 69
1. 10
2. Draw 5 cookies

Page 70
Apple and pizza can also be divided horizontally and diagonally.

Answers

Page 71

All shapes except the triangle can also be divided horizontally and diagonally.

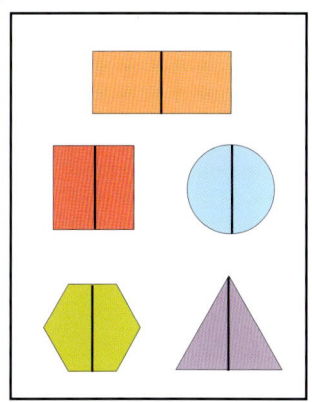

Page 72

1 bagel, 2 orange slices, 3 grape bunches, 4 pretzels

Page 73

1. 5
2. 5
3. 6

Page 74

1. 7
2. 6
3. 5

Page 75

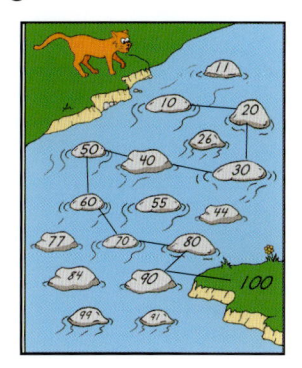

Page 76

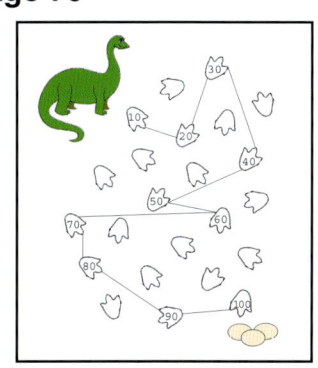

Page 77

Page 78

1. 30
2. 50
3. 50
4. 70

Page 79

1. 15
2. 30
3. 20
4. 50

Page 80

1. 8
2. 25
3. 30
4. Circle purse 3.

Page 81

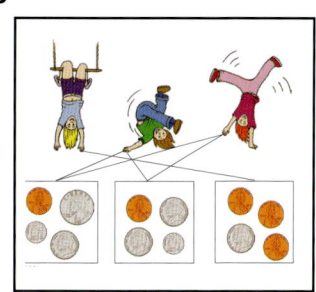

Page 82

1. quarter, 25
2. nickel, 5
3. dime, 10

Page 83

1. 15
2. 20

Page 84

1. 40
2. 50

Page 85

1. yes
2. no
3. yes

Page 86

1. 6
2. 4
3. 6
4. yes

ALGEBRA

Page 87

1. 12, 14, 15
2. 13; 16, 18; 22, 24

Page 88

1. 3
2. key box
3. 1
4. 1

Page 89

1. (triangle, oval, triangle)
2. triangle
3. triangle
4. (square, circle, circle)
5. circle
6. circle

Page 90

1. clap stomp clap stomp clap stomp clap stomp
2. clap clap stomp stomp clap clap stomp stomp
3. clap stomp stomp clap stomp stomp clap

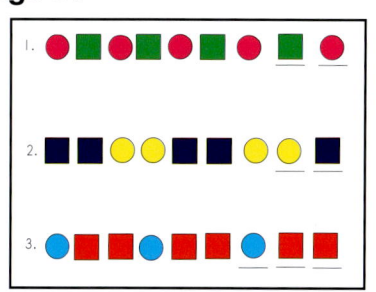

Page 91

Answers

Page 92

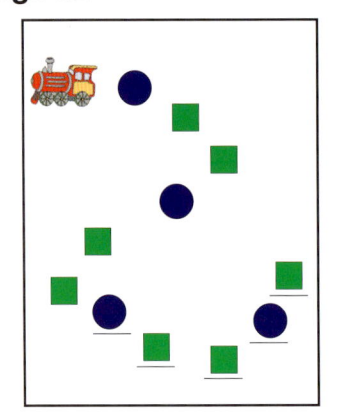

Page 93

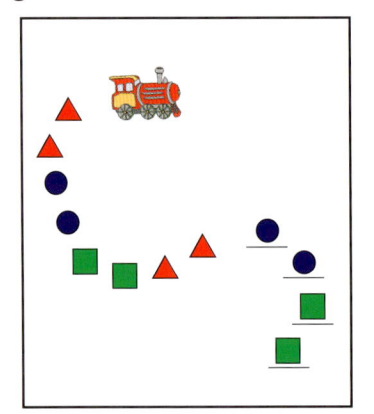

Page 94

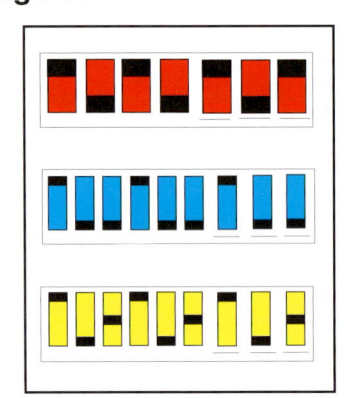

Page 95

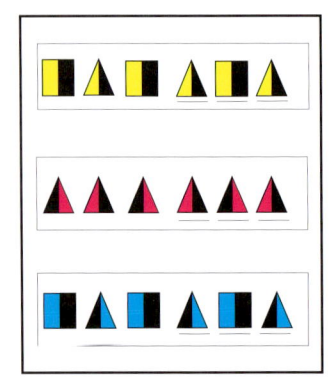

Page 96

Page 97

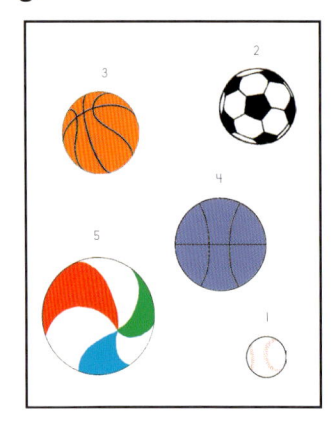

GEOMETRY

Page 98

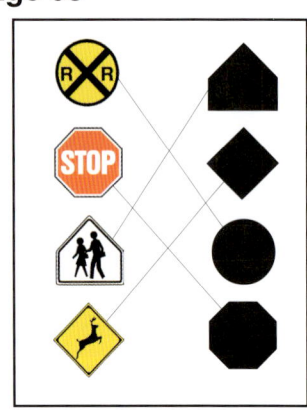

Page 99
1. 5
2. 11
3. 4-sided

Page 100
1. 6
2. 5
3. 4

Page 101
1. 5
2. 7
3. 8

Page 102

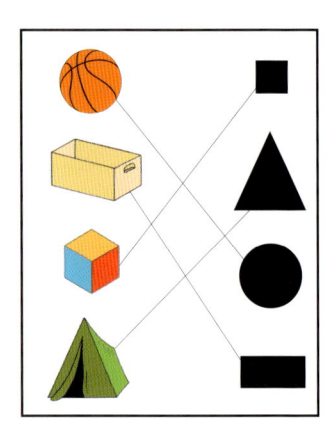

Page 103
1. circle
2. triangle
3. rectangle
4. triangle

Page 104
1. circle
2. triangle
3. rectangle
4. triangle

Page 105

Page 106

Mind Building Math — Answers

Page 107

1–2. [triangle: 3 sides; triangle: 3 sides; square: 4 sides]

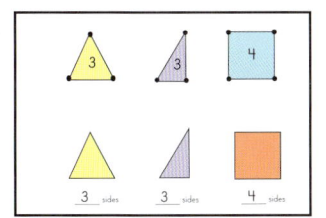

3. 4 corners

Page 108

1–2. [heptagon: 7 sides; hexagon: 6 sides; pentagon: 5 sides]

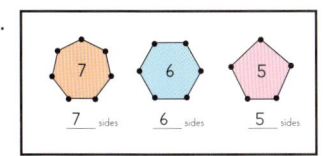

3. No. A shape always has the same number of sides and corners.
4. No.

Page 109

1. [hexagon divided into two trapezoids]
2. [triangle divided into two triangles]

Page 110

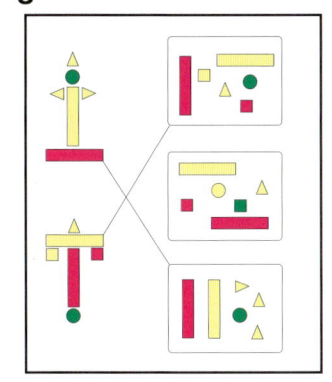

[matching figures]

Page 111

[matching figures]

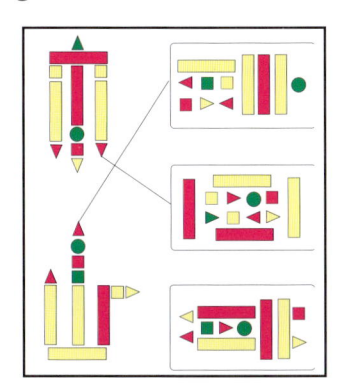

Page 112

1. rectangle
2. circle
3. Put X on the circle.
4. Circle the bottom triangle.

Page 113

1. rectangle
2. square
3. triangle
4. rectangle
5. square

Page 114

1. bucket
2. towel

[beach scene]

Page 115

1. red triangle
2. blue circle
3. red rectangle
4. red square

Page 116

1. Circle the lemonade.
2. Put X on the cookie.
3. Draw a basket.
4. Draw an apple.

Page 117

1. 7
2. 5
3. 6

Page 118

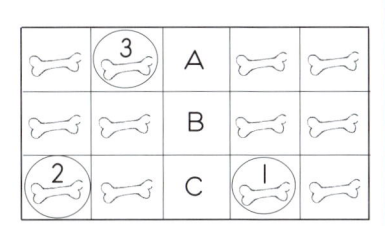

[table: bone with 3 circled, A; bone, B; 2 on bone, C, 1 on bone circled]

Page 119

1. Circle the worm.
2. Underline the ant.
3. Put X on the fly.

MEASUREMENT

Page 120

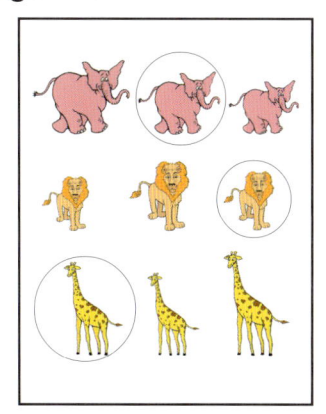

[elephants, lions, giraffes with biggest circled]

Page 121

1. red plane
2. 4
3. 2
4. blue plane

Page 122

1. suitcase
2. bath tub
3. bus

Page 123

1. more; it is bigger
2. [three containers, middle one X'd, right one circled]

Page 124

[seesaw images]

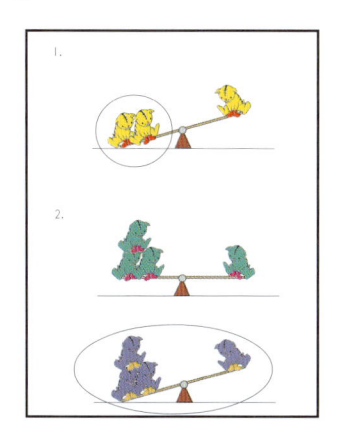

© 2004 The Critical Thinking Company • www.CriticalThinking.com • 800-458-4849

Answers

1. Two cats weigh more than one. More weight makes the side go down.
2. Three cats weigh more than one, so the left side would go down.

Page 125

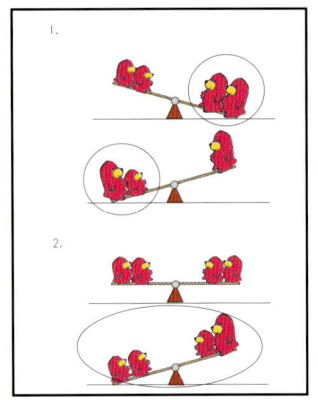

1. The side with more or bigger animals is heavier and would go down.
2. The side with more weight would go down (the large and small animals together would be heavier than two small ones).

Page 126
1. 8
2. 7
3. 3

Page 127
1. 6
2. 8
3. 3
4. Circle the frog.

Page 128
1. clock
2. thermometer
3. tape measure

Page 129
1. 12
2. 6
3. 1
4. 12
5. 5

Page 130
1. 12
2. 6

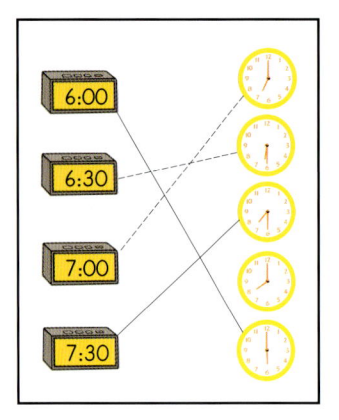

Page 131
(7:00; 7:30)
1. :00
2. :30
3. 7:00
4. 6:30

Page 132
1. Thursday
2. Friday
3. sunny
4. partly cloudy

Page 133
1. Tues
2. Sat
3. Mon
4. Tues
5. Sun

Page 134
1. swim
2. 2
3. 6
4. ride bike
5. Thursday

DATA ANALYSIS

Page 135
1. 3
2. cats
3. 2

Page 136
1. 2
2. 1

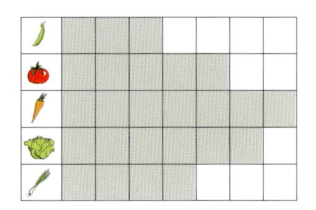

Page 137

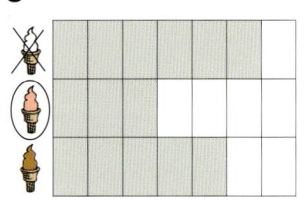

Pages 138–139
1. 6 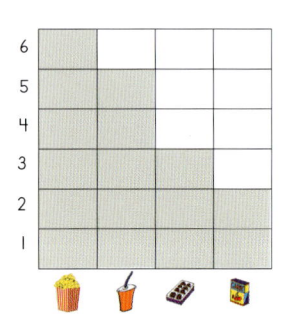
2. Circle the popcorn.
3. Put X on the cherry candy.
4. 1

Page 140–141
1. 11
2. 5
3. 4
4. 2

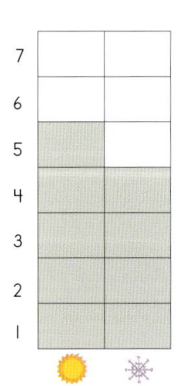

Mind Building Math — Answers

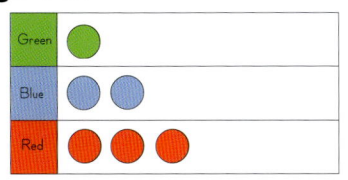

Page 142

Answers may vary but must show the fewest green balls and the most red balls.

Page 143

1. 2
2. 2
3. 2

Page 144

1. 5
2. 2
3. Jim
4. Zack

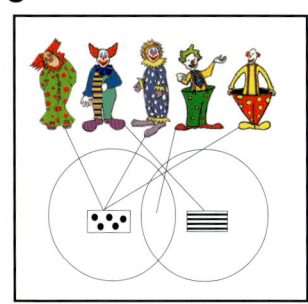

Page 145

Matrices   Mind Building Math

Skills Matrices

	1	2	3	4	5	6	7	8	9	10	11	12	13	14	15	16	17	18	19	20	21	22	23	24	25	26	27	28	29	30	31	32	33	34	35
NUMBERS AND OPERATIONS																																			
Counting	■	■	■	■	■	■	■	■	■	■	■	■	■															■		■					
Ordering Numbers														■	■	■	■																		
Ordinal Numbers																		■	■	■	■	■													
Number Words																							■												
Comparing Sets																								■	■	■	■	■	■	■	■	■	■	■	■
THINKING SKILLS																																			
Classification																																			
Comparison																								■	■	■	■	■	■	■	■	■	■	■	■
Sequencing	■	■	■	■	■	■	■	■	■	■	■	■	■					■	■	■	■	■	■	■											
Logical Reasoning								■												■													■	■	

	36	37	38	39	40	41	42	43	44	45	46	47	48	49	50	51	52	53	54	55	56	57	58	59	60	61	62	63	64	65	66	67	68	69
NUMBERS AND OPERATIONS																																		
Estimating	■	■	■																															
Grouping Objects						■	■	■	■	■	■																							
Adding/Subtracting											■	■	■	■	■	■	■	■	■	■	■	■	■	■	■	■	■	■	■	■	■	■	■	■
THINKING SKILLS																																		
Classification						■	■	■	■	■	■																							
Comparison	■	■												■	■	■	■																	
Sequencing											■	■																						
Logical Reasoning											■	■																	■					

	70	71	72	73	74	75	76	77	78	79	80	81	82	83	84	85	86	87	88	89	90	91	92	93	94	95	96	97
NUMBERS AND OPERATIONS																												
Fractions	■	■	■	■	■																							
Counting by 5s & 10s						■	■	■	■	■	■	■	■	■	■	■												
Coin Value											■	■	■	■	■	■												
ALGEBRA																												
Extending Patterns																		■	■	■	■	■	■	■	■			
Ordering Objects																											■	■
THINKING SKILLS																												
Classification											■	■	■	■	■	■												
Comparison		■	■	■	■																							
Sequencing																		■	■	■	■	■	■	■	■			
Logical Reasoning												■				■				■								

	98	99	100	101	102	103	104	105	106	107	108	109	110	111	112	113	114	115	116	117	118	119
GEOMETRY																							
Comparing Shapes	■	■	■	■	■	■	■															
Shape Attributes								■	■	■	■											
Combining Shapes												■	■	■								
Spatial Position															■	■	■					
Directions																		■	■	■	■	■
THINKING SKILLS																							
Classification								■	■	■												
Comparison	■	■	■	■	■	■	■				■	■	■	■	■	■	■	■	■	■	■	■
Sequence																						
Logical Reasoning					■				■	■		■	■									

	120	121	122	123	124	125	126	127	128	129	130	131	132	133	134	135	136	137	138	139	140	141	142	143	144	145
MEASUREMENT																											
Comparing	■	■	■	■		■																				
Measuring					■		■	■	■																	
Clock Time											■	■	■													
Calendar														■	■	■										
DATA ANALYSIS																											
Using Data																	■									
Graphing																		■	■	■						
Sorting Data/Graphing																					■	■	■			
Using Venn Diagrams																							■	■	■	■
THINKING SKILLS																											
Classification																					■	■	■	■	■	■
Comparison	■		■	■		■																				
Sequence											■		■	■												
Logical Reasoning	■				■						■	■		■	■										■	